Antique Iron

Identification and Values

Kathryn McNerney

COLLECTOR BOOKS

A Division of Schroeder Publishing Co., Inc.

The current values in this book should be used only as a guide. They are not intended to set prices, which vary from one section of the country to another. Auction prices as well as dealer prices vary greatly and are affected by condition as well as demand. Neither the author nor the publisher assumes responsibility for any losses that might be incurred as a result of consulting this guide.

Searching For A Publisher?

We are always looking for knowledgeable people considered to be experts within their fields. If you feel that there is a real need for a book on your collectible subject and have a large comprehensive collection, contact us.

Collector Books
P.O. Box 3009
Paducah, Kentucky 42002-3009

www.collectorbooks.com

Copyright © 1984 by Kathryn McNerney

Dedication

For Tom...of quiet strength

Appreciation

Permission to photograph artifacts in homes and sales displays is always a privilege -- and I am grateful. I will never forget the knowledgeable information given, physical assistance offered and truly kind interest shown by these folks. It all meant so much to me. Thank you.

Alabama

Mr. & Mrs. Milton Collins, Axis

Canada

D.K. Stewart, The Brooklin Antiquarian, Port Perry, Province of Ontario

Florida

Dot's Early Times Antiques, Milton
Country Cricket, Orange Park
Molly and Tom L. McNerney, Orange Park
Antique Boutique, Pensacola
Dennis Sullivan's Antiques, Pensacola
Hamilton House Antiques, Pensacola
Scuba Shack, Pensacola
The Loft Antiques, Pensacola
Old Sugar Mill, St. Augustine

Georgia

George R. and Dotty Fellows, Avondale Estates
Kudzu Korner, Decatur
Mr. & Mrs. Wm. A. Hicks, Decatur

Kentucky

Burwick and Merle Downs, Cadiz
Kentucky Historical Society, Frankfort
Interpretation and Environmental Education Services, Land Between the Lakes, TVA, Golden Pond

Louisiana

The Brown House, Lafayette
Wilhelmina Cook, Lafayette

Mississippi

Hunter House Antiques, Hattiesburg

Missouri

Markland's Antiques, Armstrong
Tom and Charlotte Burton, Clark
Lewis's Antiques, Clark
Dorothy Robb, Moberly
Jean Bogie, Moberly
Jim's Barn Antiques, Moberly
Sue Hartley, Moberly

New York

Carol Albesi, Lewiston Landing, Lewiston
Donna Portale, Lewiston Landing, Lewiston
Ruth Stinebring, Lewiston Landing, Lewiston
The Jolly Jester, Lewiston
Nettie Stimson, Country Barn Shop, Wilson
Red Gates Farm, Wilson
Wilson Historical Society, Wilson
Bruce, Richard, and Virginia Smithson, Youngstown
Grant and Nettie Martin, Youngstown
Old Fort Niagara Association, Youngstown
Sharon Fisher, Youngstown
Tom and Elizabeth Hooker, Youngstown

Ohio

Trash and Treasure, Ashtabula
Rose Allen, Columbus

Tennessee

Murfreesboro Antique Mall, Murfreesboro
Hazel Burch, Nashville
Gene and Marie Norris, Smyrna
Walter King Hoover, Smyrna

CONTENTS

THE CONTINUING AGE OF IRON

With his feet solidly planted on a greenish-blue slag mound, from which he liked to direct his sweating crews in their final preparations, Jake clamped his battered hat further over bushy eyebrows. Thumbs hooked under his belt to impatiently hitch up pants already jerked high, he shifted a bulging chaw of tobacco from one cheek to the other, quiet only when the temperature of the melting ore had reached his approved heat peak. Then he peered intently at the tall brick stack where the color of its rising smoke would indicate to him when to pour. Suddenly, Jake spat out his chaw, wiping his chin with the back of his hand. He threw back his head and the cry that rolled down the narrow valley was the Furnace Master's "GIVE 'ER FIRE!"

This was a weekday; fires were banked on Sundays. It was the 1850's at Center Furnace, for example, one of many built in western Kentucky and Tennessee between and along the Cumberland and Tennessee Rivers, accessible to ferries and riverboats. An earlier discovery of ore for iron and limestone for flux along with dense forests for charcoal made feasible the cold blast method of making "pigs" and had brought more settlers and jobs to this region. The shallow-based ore was dug with picks and shovels and carried to the furnace in oxcarts.

Though each had his own style of command, the heat level and call for tapping remained only with the individual Furnace Master, wherever in our richly-endowed country deposits were concentrated enough to make mining, smelting, and manufacturing financially feasible. While Saugus, Massachusetts is generally accredited with having our first successful iron works, in the mid-17th century, it was preceded by a disastrous attempt in Virginia. Workers had been protected by militiamen during several years of tremendous effort. In March, 1622, at Falling Creek near Jamestown, everyone in the settlement gathered to watch the firing of the newly completed iron furnace. At the moment of readiness, with ore and fuel aplenty and great piles of seashells for lime, Indians attacked, destroying the whole operation and killing most of the celebrants.

The Early Iron Age, following that of the Bronze, is regarded as 1500 B.C. to A.D. 100, the period in our civilization when iron weapons and tools were introduced. Bronze was available only to ruling classes; when iron came along it was available to just about everyone.

In 1400 B.C., the Hittites gained control of Asia Minor by discovering how to convert iron ore – repeatedly heating, hammering, and then dashing it into cold water (practicing the basic law of metals, that heat softens, and hammering hardens). This made possible gigantic steps in their agriculture and adornments, while with iron weapons (iron's primary purpose) they easily conquered tribes still fighting with softer bronzes. But secrets are rarely kept, and by 1200 B.C., the Hittites themselves were overcome by iron weapons in the hands of their foes.

Iron window grilles have endured in the ruins of Pompeii, so the Romans had it; ancient Egyptians wore polished beads fashioned from meteorite iron. Though human attitudes have mellowed in many parts of our world since the Early Iron Age, the strength of the iron has not. Covering about 5 percent of the earth's surface, its products have become so much a part of our living we take them for granted. So our dependency continues but in a hugely diversified manner. Iron is still the most useful, and least expensive of the "Great Metals."

Meanwhile, Center's employment had promoted a typically burgeoning furnace town (called Hematite) with adequate homes, boarding houses (charging $10.00 a week), churches, smithies, schools, and the lot. The ever-present Company Store traded workers' tokens and paper scrip for just about everything from harness to salt, boots to buttons, and candy to calico; the hands of the laborers rarely touched cash. For the entire operation, about 250 – 300 men were required, each working 12 hours a day.

Center operated from the late 1840s throughout the Civil War period, and again from 1879 to 1883. When it reopened in 1905, foremen earned $40.00 – $50.00 a month; furnacemen, $1.00 – $1.60 a day for a 12-hour shift; wood setters at the charcoal pens, $1.00 a day; wood choppers, $.50 a cord (cutting 2–2½ cords a day); ore diggers received about $1.00 for their 12-hour efforts. These wages were much less during the first two furnace activities.

Eventually, ore lying in adjacent deposits was gone. What remained in lighter amounts in scattered distances was unprofitable to mine. The unbridled cutting of timber in the area was fast leading to its total depletion. Hauling costs became prohibitive since Center had never run on a high profit margin. Richer deposits found elsewhere and competition from new processes resulted in the final abandonment of Center in 1912.

And as the last barge crowded with families and goods moved slowly into midstream, the only sound faintly drifting from the once-busy town was the creak of a splintery door held by its bent hinges, crookedly swinging back and forth, back and forth, in a ghost town already beginning to crumble into dust.

CASTING (FOUNDING)

Casting iron was the method whereby iron "pigs" were remelted and the molten metal poured into molds. Skilled pattern makers (sometimes also required to be fine carvers) made a pattern, usually in wood, from which molds were made for the actual castings. Patterns reflected the size of the object, how many were to be made (how often the mold was to be used), and if it was to be solid or one of various pieces put together. Many old 2-piece collectibles have one half with one or more tiny protruding "ears" which fit exactly into slots in the other half. On some, the line of jointure may be so expertly fashioned it is scarcely noticeable; on others it is quite evident and sometimes there is a slight gap between the parts. Permanent metal patterns could be made if many simple parts were planned, and methods of wax and pressure were developed. In the sand casting method, sand containing a binder to hold it together was packed around the pattern to make flasks suitable for smaller articles. It was necessary for the pattern to be lifted out without disturbing the molded contours in the sand. When the pattern was removed, channels or sprues were cut to the sand cavity, and molten metal was poured through the sprues. Ladles and/or small pots with or without pouring-lips could be used to fill the mold cavities with molten metal. Once the casting had solidified in the depression, it was removed, its surfaces polished, and rough edges and other irregularities smoothed. For large flat pieces, as firebacks and stoveplates, for instance, furnaces might cast on a sandcovered floor, molten metal flowing right into the cavities from the furnace. Foundries seldom used this floor method.

For a while, furnaces and foundries paralleled in types of buildings and operations, although foundries were small units, built in or near more populous areas, that worked on a daily basis. The furnace made pigs and sold them to the foundry but each cast shapes from the pigs and each actively competed for the retail trade. As markets expanded with subsequent demands for a wider range of products, furnaces became producers of pigs only while foundries bought the pigs from the thriving furnaces to supply retailers with cast shapes.

Wrought iron was fashioned by hand – heated, hammered, and beaten into forms with tools. The transition from wrought to cast iron evolved gradually from increasing labor costs and a shortage of professional craftsmen who could rapidly turn out quality items in volume. The 1830's through the mid 1850's has been called the "Great Era of Cast Iron." Victorians couldn't seem to get enough fanciful castings in truly intricate and beautiful patterns, using them indoors and out. Foundries were pressed to supply innumerable necessities while concentrating on "lacy" appendages and furniture, the makers even resorting (when orders piled up) to copying richly detailed patterns formerly used for wrought items. Walls of cavernous kitchens in mansions were literally lined with cast iron cooking vessels. Those at less affluent levels had their share on into the 1900's.

Cast iron building frames and iron bridges were produced in 1845. A cast iron building in New York City was first viewed with reservations, but led to others being constructed in many states. The Pontalba Building on Jackson Square in New Orleans was our country's first to have cast iron galleries, a feature still popular today in many areas. The discovery of gold in California brought urgent requests for easily erected durable shelters. So cast iron building parts were shipped from New York City around the Horn, each section carefully crated against dampness, the eternal enemy of iron. England entered this market but American products arrived on the West Coast faster, and were more quickly and easily assembled. The East Coast and Midwest turned out quality products in large numbers. Pennsylvania with its bountiful natural resources was the "Heartland" of cast iron productions. Along with New England, their operations were sometimes known as "Furnace Plantations."

Certain foundries specialized in their own exclusive recognizable patterns for stoves, bells, etc., while large cities ordered their own designs for sewer lids, window grilles, public fountains, benches, bird baths, etc. Downspouts in Savannah, Georgia, can still be seen gushing water from the mouths of dolphins. Railroad waiting rooms in depots might contain ponderously heavy cast iron seats – severely simple, hard and cold for travelers; others could be handsomely detailed with more gracious (and warmer) wooden seats and/or backs.

Outdoor furniture is more often seen in our southland, west coast, and southwest, where the climates have more gently affected them, and Spanish and French influences are noticeable. Countrywide, the Victorian affluence was evidenced in cast iron lawn animals, deer, dogs and the like. Castings also represented classical Greek and Roman motifs, actual and mythological, flowing draperies, flora, and fauna. So much was made, and while a decorative flourish here and there might have become broken through the years from brittle composition and general wear, with their overall ruggedness, many cast iron pieces still endure.

BUYING – CLEANING – COPIES

For some time architects and decorators have been alert to the beauty and resourcefulness of early iron castings and, along with collectors, have been searching for them; but much remains. With increasing interest in our homespun heritage, castings have emerged as important collectibles. Their darkness in tools and housewares, for example, is particularly appealing hung against lighter walls alone or combined with artifacts of other materials.

Most early foundries supplied retail trade close to home or shipped to far away places – one reason being the weight of the metal made shipping in old-timey conveyances problematic. That is not so important now with modern shipping and equipment handling; what *is* important today is the expense involved, which must be included in the cost of the item. Markets for antiques are as much affected by local and national business trends and unemployment levels as any other business. Buying practices differ countrywide; items avidly sought in one state could be ignored in the next. Heavily populated areas are bound to have more buyers and thus higher prices than more remote places. Completeness of parts, age, condition, workmanship, and touchmarks are all factors in pricing along with what the dealer has to pay. These all cause values to fluctuate. Ultimately, price is determined by what the buyer is willing to pay, within reasonable limits fair to the seller. Values herein are determined by item's owners according to all these circumstances. Treasured inherited artifacts with only sentimental value are seldom marketable. Where opinions might differ, all factors presented should be thoroughly researched.

Auctions are something else. Keen desire meets spirited, competitive bidding, often increasing a mild inclination to buy. With preparatory knowledge of what something is approximately worth, a ridiculously high figure can be spotted and a low one appreciated. Read, look closely, ask questions. When in a shop or at a show, if you are still uncertain about buying an object, ask the dealer if it is genuinely old.

A number of 19th century foundries embossed touchmarks on their wares. Along with a given name could be weight, date of patent, and pattern number. Without these it is almost impossible to find a source. Copies rarely carry the name of the maker unless on a paper label. Faded labels, fortunately, may remain on them.

Early iron castings of good quality have a character all their own. When an early item is properly cleaned, it has a beautifully soft, satiny, fine-grained, quality look, good to the touch; copies remain porous and gritty after cleaning, not good to the touch. "Repros" might have a deeper color, but remember they could have been darkened. Feel the object for smoothness of texture. Items, mostly kitchenware, have sometimes been left out in the weather, even covered with dirt, in an effort to falsify aging. The resultant furiously red overall solid rust is blatantly new, quite unlike the old naturally rusted cast iron. Old rust seems to me to be a softer reddish color and appear more in patches.

These deliberate copies are not to be confused with the new cast iron objects honestly sold as such in all kinds of shops and at flea markets. I recently saw a well cast 4-piece set of pots and skillets with lids, coarsely light gray in appearance, offered with the present manufacturer's labels at $20.00 – $40.00 a set. The instructions volunteered by the friendly flea marketeer as to "seasoning" them before usage parallels the treatment given the early cast cookware.

Unless you prefer the "as is" patina, clean off the wear and tear of years of service (maybe even exposure damage), bringing the pieces back as closely as possible to their original appearance (and usefulness if you want that, too).

It is most fortunate to have family-kept pieces. Long ago when furnaces and/or foundries were hard put to keep up with retail orders, and with quality steadily improving, people waited in lines to buy essentials such as kettles, pots, and pans. These were handled with care, passed down from one generation to another until, completely worn out, they were reluctantly consigned to the scrap pile. Since items in fairly good condition or only slightly rusted are still usable, a little going over with fine steel wool or kitchen scouring pads, wiping, applying a solid shortening, and again wiping should suffice.

It once was that newly bought cast iron cooking wares were well greased with lard, put into the oven to heat-season, then wiped and stored in the cupboard away from dampness until needed again. After using, they were carefully cleaned, maybe again wiped with an oily rag, and set back. In many homes, nevermore did that vessel touch soap and water. Undoubtedly, in other homes they were washed, then oiled and set back. It was suggested that if the old waves were not washed but kept cleaned and greased, sticking of foods would lessen and after several uses disappear altogether.

In traveling various states and in talking with innumerable dealers and collectors, I found just about as many firm opinions on how to clean old iron castings as there are serious participants. The following report of my findings carries no guarantees from me.

For those objects intended *for food contact*, careful attention should be given each piece so it will be safe to use, and at the same time, assume as closely as possible its original appearance. For normal rusting and/or heavy incrustations of grease, or where stripping is needed from a piece that has been painted,

    a. apply an oven cleaner; the alternative is to use a *fine* wire brush (hopefully attached to a power rotary wheel).

    b. wipe carefully (paper towels recommended).

    c. wipe with a light coating of mineral oil or a solid cooking shortening (some use salad oil).

    d. bake in a low heat oven, 250 to 300 degrees F., for about 15 minutes; another group advocates oven-baking for almost an hour up to 450 degrees F., this latter method turning the iron even blacker.

e. let cool; wipe carefully; piece is ready to use.

Liquid salad oils are said to be more difficult to handle than the solid shortenings and tend to smoke more heavily under heat. And if not properly wiped dry, liquid oils can become rancid on a kitchenware piece.

A cotton swab, or emery or other cloth wrapped around a small stick or toothpick dipped in oil and applied to minute and difficult to reach spots are fine for cleaning. The oil prevents scratching and softens dirt and grease.

Pieces only ornamentally intended, or to be used outside food contact (tools, sadirons, bookends, doorstops, and the like), can be cleaned with steel wool or a fine wire brush, followed by a choice of :

a. wiping with mineral oil

b. wiping with an antique-care product containing a good cleaning agent or

c. *spraying* (not brushing) with a satin finish clear lacquer-type preservative.

Sandblasting is appropriate only for very large objects. If steel wool is used, proceed carefully, as bearing down too hard could cause scratches.

If you like collectibles painted, a spray is more effective than a brush. For seriously pitted or otherwise badly worn items, this could be the only answer. It is protective on furniture and such, especially those items planned for outdoor use. White painted cast iron pieces are effective indoors or out. Naturally, painting old kitchenwares does destroy the original texture look of the casting and prohibits food contact.

FARMING

PLOW BLADE
Double Oxen; human-guided; ca. 1853 – 1830; with this a settler on the Niagara Frontier, eager to get his fields ready to plant in grain, could plow closely around stumps in that once heavily-forested area. $225.00, variable to area

PLOW BLADE
Horse-drawn, human-guided; embossed "BARNUM PLOW, WILSON, N.Y. 1856." $225.00, variable to area

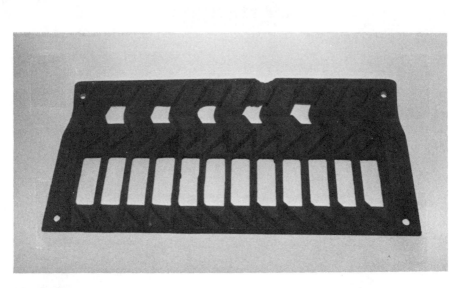

CORNSHELLER
Patent Dated February 28, 1875; used fastened to another piece of equipment. $145.00

DOUBLE HEAD WRENCH
To fit 2 size nuts on equipment; exerting a twisting strain loosened nuts, bolts, etc; embossed: 20,0 & 00,0. $55.00

Type of HIGH PRES-SURE PUMP used on horse-drawn spray rigs; 21" high x 20" wide x 15" deep. $175.00, variable to area

FAIRBANKS-MORSE GASOLINE ENGINE used on spray rigs for pumping water; ca. 1918. $175.00, variable to area

SPRAY RIG, horse-drawn; cast axles, cast and forged wheels, ca. 1890 – 1900; worker stood at rear to direct sprayer equipment; from our upper New York State "Fruit Basket." $225.00

OILSPOUT DOME and TWO LACY ENDS on red–painted wood wagon tool box; embossed both ends: WHITELY; 8½" high to top of spout, 16" long x 5¼" wide. $210.00

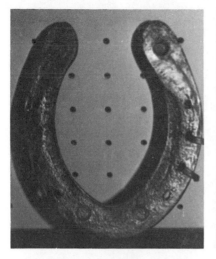

WORKHORSE SHOE
Imprinted "Patented July 23, 1912 LOCKJAW #3F"; original nails; snow and ice caulks to prevent slipping; cast shoes were heated in a forge and hammered on an anvil to fit the animal's feet. $45.00

Commercial ICE TONGS. Ice blocks cut from a northern Missouri farm pond were caught in these jaws, and with top tong's ring fastened to a heavy chain, were horse-dragged out and into a horse-drawn wagon, hauled to an icehouse and stored in sawdust; when needed, an ice pick outlined and then chipped out any desired amount; that smaller block also lifted with the tongs. $48.00

FRUIT PULPER, maker embossed; main operative parts cast; ca. latter 1800s. $245.00, variable to area

FOOD CHOPPER
Manually turned handle activates chopper inside tin tub. Blade goes up and down as tub rotates to cut food evenly; marked: "L.B. STARRETTS PATENT MAY 23 1865"; 16" x 13½". Sometimes known as a "Hasher" for meat (mfgd. by Athol Machine Co., Athol Depot, Massachusetts). $215.00

TOBACCO CHOPPER
Ca. 1840, inside wood teeth; similar to operation of sausage grinder; wood handlegrip; 4 legs stand on original walnut block. $215.00

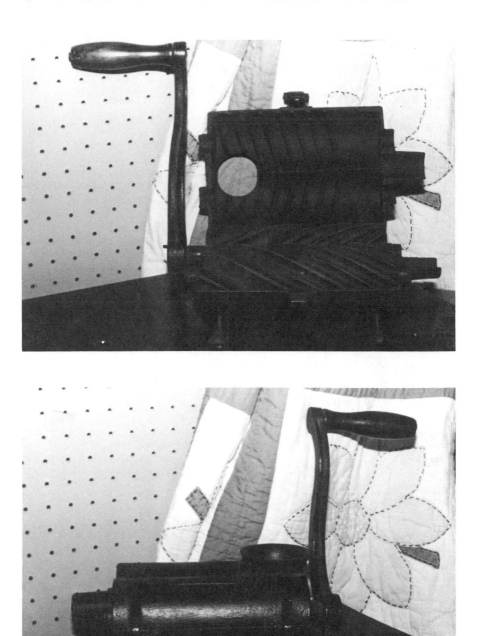

TOBACCO CHOPPER, wood handlegrip; 2 removable grinder wheels; patented 1859 March 15; style similar to sausage grinder but larger ridges here. $215.00

WINDMILL WEIGHT, ca. 1800s; approximately 9 lbs., embossed HUMMER E 184. By slowing down the blades, weight protected windmill's plunger rod from damage when wind velocity increased. Normal turning of the blades pumped the water and pulled it up. $575.00 up. If painted original colors, $750.00 up

BARN DOOR HINGES
32" length; hinged at shaped section. $110.00 pair

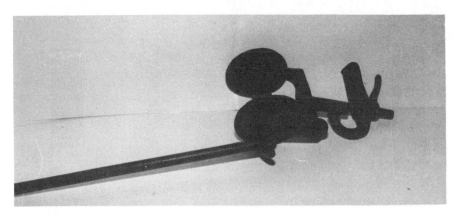

POST WINCH
Marked: PAT. SEPT. 21, '86. For hauling hay to top of barn. $85.00

Rope Sliding BARNLOFT (Haymow) HAYLIFT moved the bales from the wagon to be piled in the loft for storage. $85.00

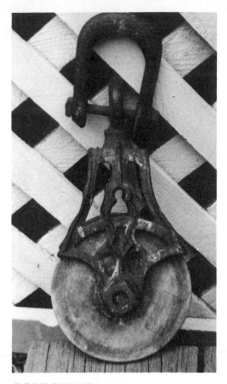

PLANTATION BELL
Graceful casting; used to summon workers, meals, alarm calls, etc. $475.00 +

ROPE PULLEY
Imprinted: F.E.M. & Bros. $48.00

SAP SPIGOTS
for New England sugar maple trees; could be hung by a pin in eye ring; was tapped by prong end into a small gash in tree; sap flowed down trough in center of spigot into bucket hanging from lower hook. $29.00 each

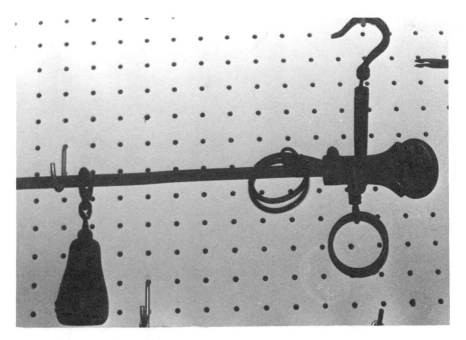

OFF CENTER BALANCE SCALE
Style in use since England's reign of Edward IV; made in many sizes; arm is the "yard" and the sliding weight the "pea." $145.00, values also variable to size

COTTON or BEAM BALANCE SCALE WEIGHTS. One at end was lead-wrapped to achieve accurate balance; 2 handles were smithy added. $100.00 – $135.00. Separate weights scarce.

BALL WEIGHT with handle; approximately 11 lbs. $100.00

SCALE WEIGHTS
1- embossed: 2 lbs., W.E. SIDDONS $95.00
1- embossed: 2 lbs., CRANE NO. 1 WOLVERHAMPTON, 3¾" dia. x 1¼" deep $95.00
1- smallest with 2" diameter x ½" deep $50.00
1- tall COTTON SCALE WEIGHT about 4 lbs. $125.00

HORSE ANCHORS: Ca. 1870s; Round – $95.00, Oblong – $95.00

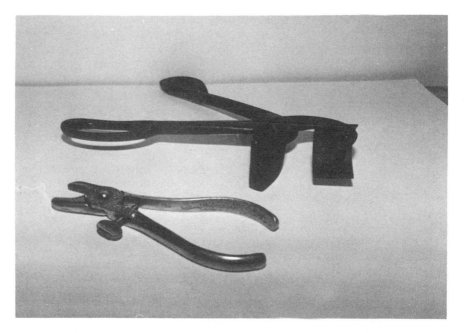

Smaller Tool – HOG RINGER to put rings through a hog's nose; marked: HILL'S HOG RINGER, PAT. AUG. 1872; screw adjustment. $65.00
Larger Tool – HOG TRIMMER for trimming the snouts of swine to keep them from rooting; ca. 1870s. $65.00

HITCHING WEIGHT, (BLOCK, HORSE ANCHOR) with rare brass studded original leather strap; carried in vehicle, set on ground with end of strap (usually a rope) fastened at bridle to keep animal from wandering off when no tree or hitching post was handy; heavy: a horse could sometimes drag one – but not far; 4" x 5"; strap 70" length. $145.00

HORSE ANCHORS
Ca. 1870 – 1880. $95.00
Large ring top. $125.00

HORSE ANCHOR
Made from a RR Spike driven into a cannonball by smithy; ca. 1800s. $75.00 +

CARRIAGE STEP
Patterned cutout cast plate; side supports smithy joined; bolted on carriage at an angle so foot could be balanced; ca. 1870; forged and other wrought parts were combined with castings. $48.00

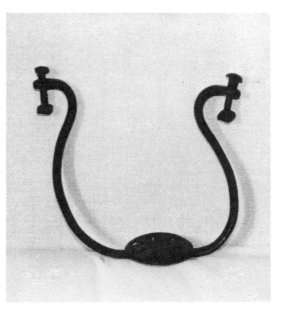

SUGAR KETTLE
Known as the famous "Kelly Kettle," introduced by William Kelly in the 19th century and sold principally to southern planters for use in processing cane; this an original kettle. $495.00 up

SUGAR KETTLE
These originals all have wide flat rims; here cleverly mounted atop cutoff southern columns. $650.00 up (kettle only)

SMALL APPLEBUTTER KETTLE (had been a planter); ring to hang on a support (cradle); heavy iron bail. Two fireplace pothooks improvised as a handle. $75.00 variable

LARGER APPLEBUTTER KETTLE
Has ears, but bail missing; 3 feet intact. $210.00

**YARD KETTLE
(APPLEBUTTER or LARD)**
Ca. late 18th century. Original wrought stand; sloping sides; heavy bail; 3 short feet intact; (sometimes on early ones the feet are burned down to stubs, or nearly so), note rim treatment. $1,100.00 variable

YARD KETTLE
Ca. latter 1700s – early 1800s. Complete with original wrought stand; rarely longer feet for fireplace cookery; restored bail. $900.00 up

YARD KETTLE
Ca. 1700s; might also have been fireplace used; handle ear one side only; (misc. tools and frogs part of owner's display). $650.00 up

HOG SCALDER KETTLE
17" deep x 27" diameter; heavy with bulge bottom; large ears each side so kettle could be set on a cradle; used at butchering time on the farm, on an autumn day cold enough to make the fingers ache and the nose red but fine to keep the meat fresh during outdoor processing. Kettles were made in many sizes, from teakettles to those on whalers, and from distilleries to boilers for tallow chandlers. $750.00 – 1,000.00

FURNITURE

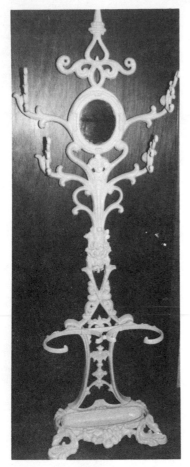

HALL TREE DRIP PANS
8½" each oval; embossed: M & H
SCHRENKEISEN, New York; for
double type hall tree. $85.00 pair

HAT and UMBRELLA STAND
5'¾" high x 26" wide; complete as original including
mirror and drip pan; ca.
1840; white painted; mint
condition. $2,500.00 variable

BOOKSTAND (HOLDER)
36" high x 19" wide; iron
rollers; adjustable heights and
book positions; ca. 1890s.
$168.00

UMBRELLA STAND (HOLDER)
27" high x 13" wide x 10" deep;
ca. 1870s; rococo Victorian;
swirled ring for easier carrying.
$285.00

FIRESIDE TOOLS STAND
(Or could be used for umbrellas
as desired); ca. 1880s; ornately
patterned. $285.00

THE ORIGINAL CAST IRON BED
67" high x 58" wide; restored black enamel with brass center rod; base not shown but available; top corners end in lions' mouths. Complete unit $975.00 up

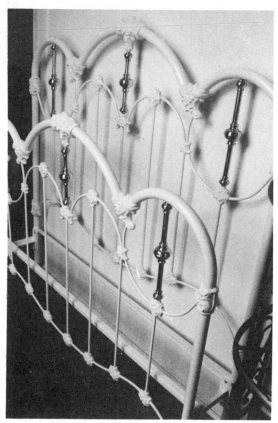

THE REPRODUCED WHITE FINISHED CAST IRON BED
With brass decorative rods; price has risen since this was produced early in 1982. $900.00 up

CRADLE
Victorian, painted white.
$695.00 up

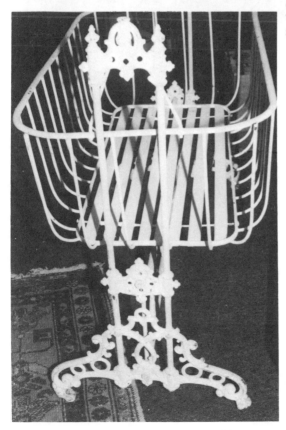

INVALID'S CHAIR

Stamped: **MARKS ADJUSTABLE CHAIR CO. NEW YORK, U.S.A. PAT'D.**; quartered oak frames, eye caning restored to original; 6 positions; flat, folding and rocking, plus 3 leg and back adjustments. When castings became so popular here a century ago in what came to be known as "Ferromania," from 1850 into the 1870's, cast iron grew into full furniture status from previously simply decorating or strengthening other materials. $775.00 and more to area.

MAGAZINE RACK
Chanticleer (Crowing Cock) in rococo pattern.
$195.00

PLANT STAND
Fluted column on 3-way ornately embossed base; 23" height; thumb screw adjusts round walnut top up or down; painted white.
$135.00 +

SCHOOL SCHOOL DESK
Principally cast iron with maple wood; 25" high;
embossed: BUFFALO, N.Y. $175.00 variable

SCHOOL DESK
Maple with equal parts
cast iron; 19th century;
23⅔" high; lifttop.
$225.00 variable

ORGAN STOOL
Heavy cast base with original upholstered revolving seat; ca. 1880 – 1890. $250.00 +

PIANO STOOL
Turntop; ornate cast base, wrought twisted iron. $195.00 +

GARDEN FURNITURE
Victorian, shown with pattern closeup:
Settee: 28½" high x 36½" wide x 13" deep
Table: 13½" high x 20" diameter
Chairs: 31" high x 13½" diameter seats
Swirls, leaves, pineapples, berries, classical figures were typical themes from the early 1800s into the 1930s. Then they were copied in a lightweight metal with far fewer intricate details. Breaks in old furniture castings are not unusual since castings could become brittle if allowed to cool rapidly in the molds; as one Penny Bank and Toy collector commented, "break like glass if you drop it." Robt. Wood & Co. in Philadelphia actively produced many styles, shipping countrywide, parts to be assembled by bolts or screws (those also cast) at destination; values vary greatly. $1,000.00 per set to over $1,800.00 per set depending upon area and existing conditions

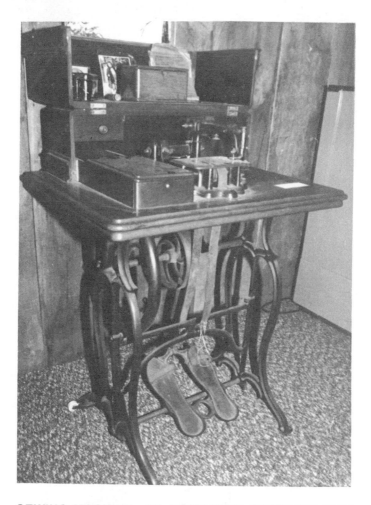

SEWING MACHINE with RARE IRON SEPARATE FEET instead of more common foot treadle platform; 36" high x 25" wide x 19" deep; Stamped with original labels: WHEELER & WILSON, PAT'd . 1850, International Pattern; this brand is the first fully operable mechanical home sewing machine available in our country; walnut top, attachments box, needle case, and top of machine cover. $795.00 – $875.00

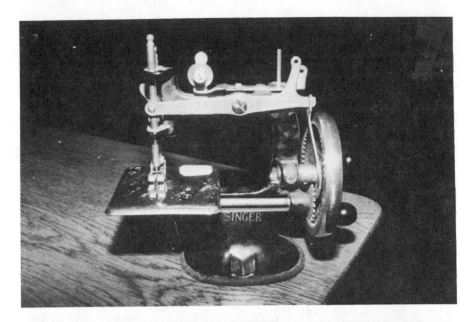

SEWING MACHINE
Japanned finish with gold striping; original labels; hand operated by turning wood knobbed side wheel; FOR ADULT USAGE: ca. 1920 – 1940; complete and operable. Paper packaging box printed: "A SINGER FOR THE GIRLS – This is Not a Toy but a Real Sewing Machine – Teaches Them to Make Clothes for Their Dolls."; mint condition. $225.00 variable

SEWING MACHINE
Small portable, manually turned wood handgrip side wheel; black japanned finish, gold stencilling; original label: EMPIRE COMPANY, dated 1860; 10½" wide x 7½" high x 7" deep, claw feet. $235.00

SEWING MACHINE
6½" high x 6" wide; original SINGER label; worn japanned black finish, gold trim; needs work to be operable. $65.00 as is

NEW SEWING MACHINE
Jr. Model NP-1; label: GATEWAY, Chicago, Ill., Patent Pending; operable.
$95.00

To illustrate how two sides of sewing machine base often seen sitting outside flea markets can be utilized: NEW HOME MACHINE base attractively patterned, iron rollers; repainted to original black with spray enamel. Top is new composition marble chips. $110.00 base only

KITCHEN and PANTRY

ATLAS STOVE (KITCHEN RANGE/COOKSTOVE)
Has attached swinging side trivets above 6 burners, left front burner with 3 graduated size plates for various degrees of heat; water reservoir; upper shelf preceded the warming oven; originally the stovepipe went through the middle of the tall post and upper shelf (could now be so used); ornate over-all designs and gracefully curved legs; nickel-plated trims contrast nicely with the black. Founding began in America about the mid-1720s, but stoves were considered only supplements to fireplace cooking. After the Revolutionary War the English 10-plate stove replaced the earlier Dutch-type 5-plate, but it was not until the 19th century that coal-burning stoves with removable burner lids achieved full individual status as cooking elements. Additional styles were cast for the prime purpose of heating, as base burners/parlor stoves. $2,000.00 – $2,800.00

RUGBY HOUSEHOLD KITCHEN RANGE with enlargement of front maker's plate; elaborate cast designs; silver paint newly emphasizes parts where nickel-plating had worn thin; 6-burner (cooking plate surfaces); stovepipe came out at center top at opening covered by coffee pot in picture; top warming shelf preceded warming ovens. $1825.00 variable

STOVE, 2-burner, NO. 8M, ATLANTA, FRANKLIN; and at the base edge: ATLANTA STOVE WORKS (Georgia). Fueled by coal and/or wood, fires usually started with paper and kindling; stovepipe rose through top rear; (Benjamin Franklin invented his first stove in 1743, and by the 1830s many cast iron models were winning over fireplaces.) These small stoves could warm at least 1 room and provide a cooking surface. $250.00

GEM STOVE NO. 80 ready to use; ca. earliest 1920s; 2½" wide x 20" deep x 22" high; turning fancy-head fingergrip side screw opened inside plates to let ashes or coal bits drop into base pit for removal; front sliding panel controlled air circulation (and thus heat degree). $225.00

STOVE (Potbelly)
Embossed: STATION
AGENT on circular top
rim; made by Union Stove
Works, New York, USA.
25½" top diameter x 46½"
high. $625.00 variable

POTBELLY STOVE
Embossed: BURNSIDE No.
20A, ENTERPRISE; 48"
high; uncommon style.
$425.00 – $575.00+

BASEBURNER
Restored to original finishes; when made had mica (isinglass) inside the door panels through which the flames beautifully flickered. $975.00 up

SALESMAN'S SAMPLE STOVE (GAS) Embossed on front: ROYAL; all original with skillet, griddle, and handled pot. $595.00 up, the set

PARLOR STOVE
GEM NO. 15, Patented 1871
Embossed: John F. Rath-
bone & Co. Albany, New
York. 38" high x 27" deep;
classic columns and floral
detail. $850.00 up

PARLOR STOVE with
detachable top urn; 32"
high # 24. $750.00 up

PARLOR STOVE
Marked on side: PEORIA; round, wood burning; stylized leaf and swirl designs with much detail; now in use. $1,800.00 – $2,000.00 +

B & H RADIANT HAND-WARMER STOVE (Cool Morning Stove) No. 6, Pat. dated: June 8, 1893 – June 12, 1894. 33" high x 16" wide; all original; burned kerosene. $550.00

CHILD'S STOVE (it really cooks, not called a toy) 20½" wide x 10" deep x 21" high; with stovepipe going up the back as on full-size ranges, coming out at the center of the top warming shelf. The stove would be fully operable as original; 6 top plates, water reservoir, swinging trivet at front, shelf to handle vessels, and equipped with a teakettle and various cookwares; rare, ca. latter 1800s. $825.00 +

STOVE PLATE
Embossed: WEIR STOVE CO. TAUNTON, MASS. $135.00

STOVE PLATE
Embossed: Wild Turkey
and Trees design; 5"
round. $150.00

WASHBOILER HOLDER
to set on stove while water in boiler is heating; pouring lip for overflow;
heavy lift/hang handles. $40.00

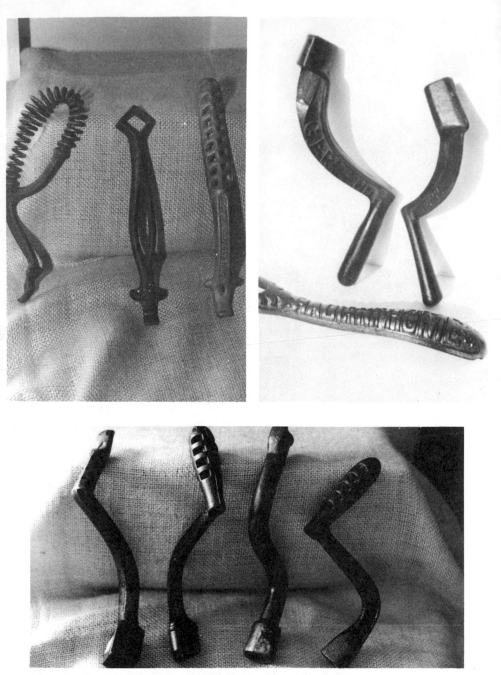

STOVE LID LIFTERS for flat stove lids. $35.00 – $40.00 ea
STOVE ASH & CLINKER SHAKERS. $38.00 – $42.50 ea
Lifters embossed: SPERITY at center; JEWEL openwork handle; IDEAL
twisted wire handle. Ca. 1890. Shakers embossed: GARLAND, EAGLE,
RADIANT HOME (lying flat) nickelplated; others not marked.

SADIRON
First known as a "sadiron," "sad" being the obsolete word for "solid," next termed a "flatiron"; now we simply call them "irons." The earliest carry no marks of identification. Later they appeared with patents, weights, dates, and/or maker, many patented by mid-1800s; sadirons were the heaviest, to smooth coarser, rougher, heavier fabrics. Here the original handle was replaced by an unusual wide, flat handle, creatively center-joined with a rosette; ca. 1830 – 1840. $95.00

SADIRON
Both handle and base were cast and then wrought together; 1800s. Stones were the first smoothing artifacts, rubbed back and forth over the damp cloth. Note whorled handle bases. $150.00 – $175.00

IRONS
Left: Smallest with open handle holes for cooling; embossed #12 OBER Pat. Pend. $95.00
Center: Embossed: ENTERPRISE MFG. CO., PHILA. U.S.A.; center STAR and PATd. October 1, '87; gracefully fluted handle, smith attached. $125.00
Right: Turkish turned-up-toe with beading on lovely handle cast separately and then forged together. $150.00

TAILOR'S SADIRON
Ponderous, smithy twisted and forged-on handle; 1800s. $95.00

TAILOR'S PRESSING IRON (GOOSE)
Blacksmith twisted and forged-on handle; ca. 1820 – 1840. $125.00+

TAILOR'S PRESSING IRON (GOOSE)
Originally named for the shape of its handle. Smith twisted and forged-on handle; ca. earliest 1800s. $125.00 – 150.00

BOX IRON, sometimes called a SLOG IRON
Once extensively used by hatters; wrought handle; ca. 1700s. Door at back opens into a hollow space for holding hot coals, or more tidily, a slog of iron already separately heated atop the stove. $325.00 up

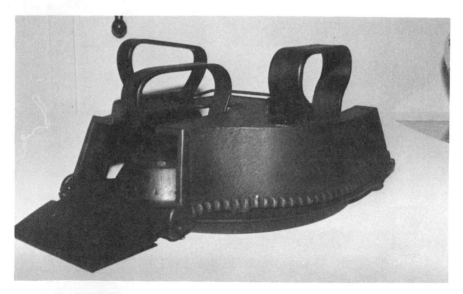

SADIRON HEATER
Shown here holding 3 sadirons (with handles sticking up); the irons customarily used in 3's, 1 in use and 2 heating; the whole set on top the stove; has 3 drop-door compartments; interesting to see the pretty bead trimming on this type of pantry piece; ca. 1870s. $350.00

"MRS. POTTS'" SADIRON SET
Interchangeable handle between 2 size irons; advertised in Sears Roebuck
Catalog for 1908 as "Her Patent" @ $.78 a Set; also shown with handle and
3 irons (usually sold as set of 3, so 1 iron could be used as others heated
on the stove) @ $3.00 a set, nickel-plated. $125.00 – $145.00

(CRIMPING) ROCKING IRON; imprinted bottom of corrugated base: PATd. Aug. 21, 1866; plate heated on stove; top inside curve embossed: GENEVA (Illinois) HAND FLUTER – in tiny beading frame. $245.00 up

ROLLER IRON; moved by its handle in corrugated ridges to pleat and crimp materials; heated plate was inserted into base slot; imprinted on base: PATd. 1880; imprinted on plate: HEATER – PUT THIS ON TOP OF STOVE. $165.00 up

FLUTER
Corrugated inside both top and bottom hinged parts; released to open by center thumb latch; Patd. Dec., latter 1800s. $295.00 +

SADIRON HEATER
Imprinted: Pat'd. June 21, 1911; placed atop the stove, sadirons on top of the heater to heat or keep warm for pressing. $125.00

TRIVETS

Wrought in the 1700s into the earliest 1900s, trivets were in full production as castings by 1850, in countless designs. The smaller were shaped to hold flatirons, the others set near or in the warm hearth ashes (or coals) were intended for holding pots and kettles, keeping their food contents heated. Flat-tops with 3 legs could sit evenly on the rough hearth; 4 legs would not sit evenly. Trivets are heavily reproduced in most of the old patterns, often difficult to recognize as new. But if the name of the trivet pattern is embossed or imprinted on the back, it isn't an old one.

TRIVET
For sadirons, embossed: "I WANT U" COMFORT IRON, STRAUSE GAS IRON CO., PHILA, PA. U.S.A. 3 legs. $150.00

TRIVET
For sadirons, embossed: "I WANT U" COMFORT IRON, STRAUSE GAS IRON CO., PHILA, PA. U.S.A. 4 legs. $145.00

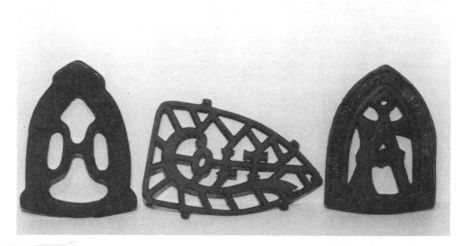

For Sadirons: H TRIVET, 3 legs, Embossed: W.H. HOWELL CO., GENEVA, ILL. $75.00; "COLT" TRIVET, 4 legs. $75.00; A F TRIVET Embossed: AMERICAN FOUNDRY & MFG. CO. ST. LOUIS, MO. 3 legs, $80.00

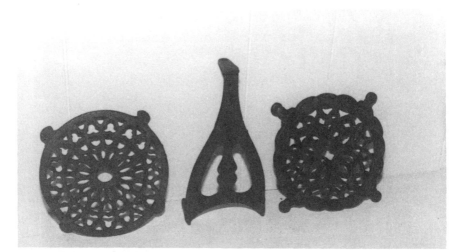

TRIVETS 4-footed ROUND $60.00; Uncommon one for SADIRON, 3 legs, $95.00; ROUND 4-footed, larger. $60.00

EAGLE TRIVET. Heavily copied. $50.00; Two HEART TRIVETS. $75.00 each;
Fourth HEART TRIVET. $125.00

For Sadirons
STAR TRIVET Embossed:
THE CLEVELAND FOUNDRY
CO. $75.00; LATTICE TRIV-
ET. $45.00

"FAMILY TREE"
Heavily copied, $45.00

**SADIRON TRIVET embossed: ENTER-
PRISE MFG. CO. PHILA. U.S.A. $95.00**

TRIVET, FRUITS and FLOWERS. $95.00; FANCIFUL. $75.00

TRIVETS
Left: CUPIDS. $95.00 – 125.00
Center: Embossed: "Jenny Lind" above handle. $145.00
Right: SQUARE with Grape Clusters signed "Wilton."
$85.00

TRIVETS: HEART-SHAPED "WILTON." $85.00
FILIGREE WITH FLOWERS IN CENTER. $75.00

TRIVET Imprinted: DUBUQUE POTTS (Iowa). $95.00

TRIVET for food containers. Ornate Gothic style; has an underneath catch believed to operate as a swinging trivet for a teakettle. $145.00

TRIVET for hot cookware. Imprinted: THE GRISWOLD MFG. CO. ERIE, PA., U.S.A. 8 TRIVET 206, 7¾" diameter. $35.00

TEAKETTLE
Ca. latter 1700s – early 1800s; gooseneck spout; handsome finial; wrought handle added. Every household had to have something in which to hold and heat water, teakettles were essential. $225.00

TEAKETTLE
Ca. 1880s; cast in 2 pieces with spout half of each; could fit into cookstove well; flat ½" wide wrought handle; sliding lid with steamhole vent; marks on inside lid not legible; very heavy – 5½ lbs.; 11" wide to end of spout; 7" wide tapering to 6¼" diameter base; Savery & Co. of Philadelphia for many years were large producers. $185.00 – $195.00

SALESMAN'S SAMPLE TEAKETTLE
5" high; liftlid with small bar finial; brass bail; maker marked: BASTER KYLE & CO. #8, LOUISVILLE, KY. June 28, 1888. $225.00 up

TEAKETTLE
14" diameter overall without wrought handle; embossed: WOOD BISHOP & CO., BANGOR, ME.; sliding lid; ca. 1800s. $185.00 variable to area

TEAKETTLE
Embossed: TERSTEGGE, GOHMANN & CO., NEW ALBANY, IND. 1883; 7¾" high, new wire bail; 12" across with spout; half-covered lip. $145.00 to area

Popularity of FOOD CONTACT COOKWARES and MOLDS is especially noticeable in Mid-America west and east of the Mississippi. Objects are still fairly plentiful and prices slightly lower in states not yet so active. Uncommon forms are sought. There were innumerable producers earlier and at the same time, but these seem to be among the favored embossings or imprintings of many searching for these collectibles: G.F. Filley, Wagner Ware (still in business) Sidney, O., and Griswold Mfg. Co., Erie, Pa. (after manufacturing a line of cookwares in Erie for many years, Griswold was sold, continuing its operations under its own name at Sidney, but as a division of Textron Industries, Inc.). Known as MUFFIN IRONS are those actually shaped for baking them, but also including irons for cinnamon treats, tea and/or party pastries, popovers, and such, while STICK PANS cover those for pone/cornbread, etc. The names may differ in areas but basically all agree as to purposes, turning out goodies. And "back then," busy cooks undoubtedly improvised, reaching for any close suitable pan rather than stopping and hunting for the "proper" vessel stashed away somewhere.

SANTA CLAUS CAKE MOLD
Embossed: HELLO KIDDIES!!! GRISWOLD MFG. CO. ERIE, PA. 2-part mold; heavy side rings. $495.00

69

LAMB CAKE MOLD
One of the best known; 2-part; ca. 1880. $165.00

Repro LAMB CAKE MOLD, ca. 1950s. $45.00

HOLDER for BAKED POTA-TOES (TONGS) Rare; petal-shaped grips. $115.00

PIG MOLD
For Souse (a pudding of lightly pickled pork bits) very heavy; many copies but without details; even painted, repros have a gritty texture; note tiny tusks here. $195.00

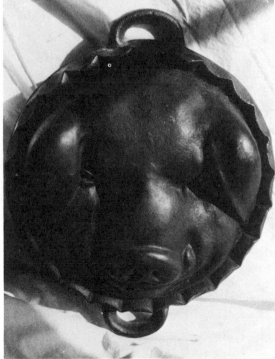

SPRINGERLE IRON
12 designs, including pear, oak leaf, turkey, grapes, baskets, horseshoe, horn of plenty. 10" high; imprinted: WAGNER WARE, SIDNEY, O.; used by pressing into dough to make the patterns, cookies cut to separate along ridges; ca. mid-1800s; a rarity. $325.00

SPRINGERLE IRON
5½" x 2¾"; floral design. $195.00

9-HEART IRON, wide bars. $165.00; 6 HEARTS and STAR center without handle, carrying ring. $145.00; 6-HEART IRON, wide carrying and hanging bar. $145.00; 4-HEART IRON with handle. $110.00; 12-HEART IRON, wide bar that is center fastened. $225.00

The collector-inheritor of these beautiful pieces considers them baking irons since her Tennessee mother always so used them; another collector described them as SUGAR MOLDS; both are acceptable descriptions.

THREE G.F. FILLEY MUFFIN IRONS
Left: 11-mold #8. $145.00. Center: 11-mold #7. $125.00. Right: 14-mold #12. $150.00.

MUFFIN, CHOCOLATE or SUGAR MOLD
Unusual pattern; hanging bar at only one end – small lift extension at other. $185.00

MAPLE SUGAR MOLD
8 Fruit and Vegetable sections; WIDELY SOUGHT; 20" x 8"; well designed handle bars. $250.00

CHOCOLATE MOLD
2 parts; 3 hands and wrists; V. CLAD & SONS, PHIL. PA. $175.00

BRIDGE PAN
10" long x 8½"
wide; double fin-
ger holds; for
party treats.
$225.00 up

**LITTLE SLAM
BRIDGE PAN**
Imprinted: WAGNER
WARE, SIDNEY, O.
#1340; hearts, dia-
monds, spades,
clubs; 11" long x 8"
wide; for party pas-
tries. $250.00

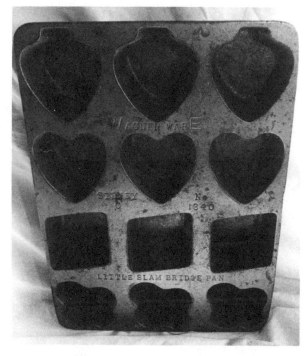

MUFFIN IRON (PARTY PASTRIES)
Beautiful casting; 12-mold fluted hearts, tarts, and doughnut shapes; ca. 1870 with Victorian ornate handles. $275.00 +

MUFFIN IRON (PARTY PASTRIES)
Hearts, stars, plain and fluted tarts; eye rings; embossed on handles: July 10, 1871. $275.00 up

MUFFIN IRON
8-mold; an especially sought rarity; base shown; 14½" x 6½"; imprinted: G.F.FILLEY NO. 4; eye bars. $210.00 +

MUFFIN IRON
14 round cups; eye bar handles; imprinted: G.F. FILLEY #12. $220.00 +

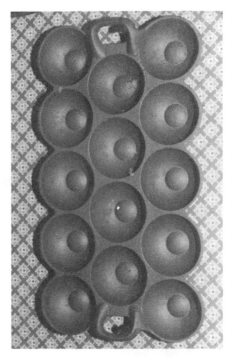

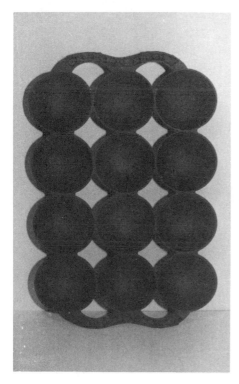

MUFFIN IRON
Round cups with row cutouts and open handles; dated April 5, 1856; uncommon. $235.00

MUFFIN OR ROLLS IRON
Flat sections; ca. 1870s; much older than usually found; imprinted: GRIS-WOLD MFG. CO. ERIE, PA. U.S.A. 946. $150.00 up

CINNAMON CRISP IRONS
Undersides to better show patterns; larger 11-forms – #30 10" x 7"; smaller 11-forms; both WAGNER WARE, SIDNEY, O; made pretty swirls on pastries. $175.00 each – more in some areas

6 Sections in a similar pattern MUFFIN IRON 9½" x 5½"; tiny eye rings. $145.00

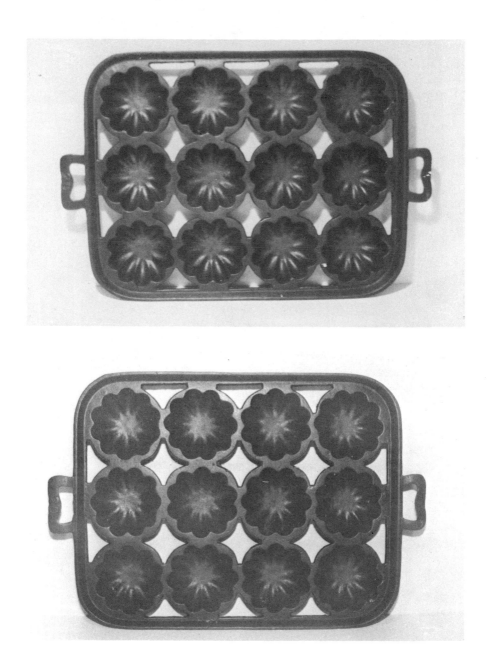

MUFFIN IRON
Top and bottom shown; 12 sections with fluted sides, scalloped top edges, flower-like; 16" x 11"; prettily shaped handle bars. $250.00 and more to area

POPOVER PAN
Cpa. 1890s; on base imprinted: No. 10 GRISWOLD, ERIE. PA. U.S.A. 948; 11" x 7½" x 1¾" deep; 11 sections. Popovers are a light pastry supposed to "pop over" the sides of the cup; 2 fingergrips. $125.00 up

4-Section IRON, flat mold $55.00

PASTRY IRON
Eye handle cutouts; muffin or flat teacakes type. $75.00+

MUFFIN IRON (PASTRIES)
Embossed: W.O. Davis & Co., CINTI, O.; heavy eye ring handles. $245.00

ROLLS PAN (MUFFIN IRON)
Much older type; ca. 1870; #3; base shown. $175.00

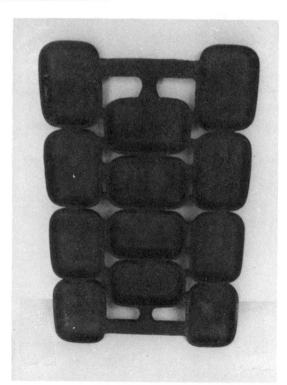

**MUFFIN, ROLLS, OR
PASTRIES IRON**
Cutouts; #20; ca. 1870;
base shown. $150.00 –
$175.00

VIENNA ROLL BREAD PAN NO. 26 Maker: GRISWOLD MFG. CO.
ERIE, PA. 958. $135.00 – $155.00

**VIENNA ROLL BREAD
PAN**
12" high x 7" wide; 2 sections bar joined top and
bottom. $150.00 +

STICK PAN
Imprinted on base: JUNIOR KRUSTY KORN KOBS Reg. in U.S. PAT. OFF. PAT'd. July 6, 1920 WAGNER WARE SIDNEY O. 1319D Rarity – 7 ears cast in reverse to each other; K letters are 3 ears of corn each. $150.00 +

FRENCH ROLL PAN
Ca. 1870's; pretty handles. $100.00 +

Front plain and back imprinted: STICK PAN, GRISWOLD CORN BREAD PAN, 954 E; "ERIE, PENN. U.S.A."; 2 rolled handles with eye rings; owners term this "common" which I interpret to mean "plentiful"; seems a good place for a beginning collector to start and should be well priced. 95.00 var

WHOLE WHEAT GRAINS STICK PAN; #639; GRISWOLD MFG. CO. ERIE, PA. #28; mostly for cornbread; A RARITY; eye ring only at larger solid bar handle end. $250.00 up

STICK PAN
Small mold much sought; 4¼" wide x 8½" long; Imprinted on back No. 262, GRISWOLD CRISPY CORN OR WHEAT STICK PAN, ERIE, PA. U.S.A. 625; 2 handles overall cast – 1 with eye ring; 7 sticks; well kept, ready to use. $150.00 +

5-STICK PAN...SCARCE
9" x 6½"; note ears are reversed – alternating stalk and cob ends; eye rings. $165.00. Center: 7-STICK PAN 12" x 5½"; eye rings; ears all facing same direction. $150.00. Largest at end: 7-STICK PAN 12½" x 5¾"; ears again in reverse; larger individual ears; eye rings. $195.00

CLOSEUP of 7-STICK PAN, cobs in reverse; note casting attention given the grains.

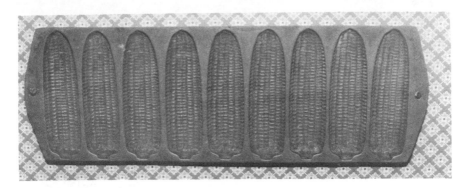

9-STICK PAN
Eye rings; looks nice on the wall. $195.00

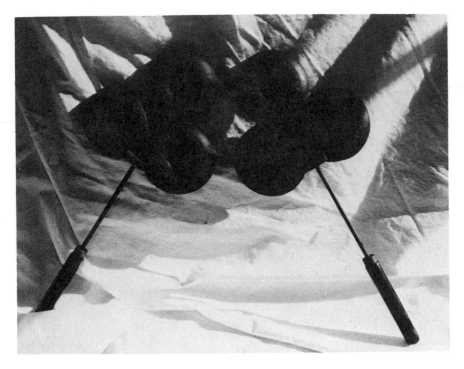

DOUGHNUT MOLD (FRYER)
Makes 3 at a time; 2 parts with 2 hinges; long handles; embossed: ACE
CLOVERLEAF DONUT. $145.00

DOUGHNUT IRON BAKER'S HALF DOZEN Open handles; dated Dec. 1870. $185.00

FRENCH WAFFLE IRON for 2 cakes. Embossed: PAT. JUNE 29, 1880 SELDEN & GRISWOLD: STAR: 2 hinged parts; 12" long x 4" diameter; originally may have had wood handles — or iron. $155.00

WAFFLE IRON
Handles wrought and forged on; ca. 1790. $200.00 –
$275.00 up

WAFFLE IRON and STAND
Embossed: THE WAGNER
MFG. CO., SIDNEY, O.
PAT'd. FEB. 22, 1910.
Turned by wood handle to
bake both sides; stand has
carrying bail. $135.00

TURNTABLE WAFFLE IRON Embossed: NEW AMERICAN #8 GRISWOLD
PATENTED MAY 14 and 21, 1901, OTHERS PENDING. Wood handles,
designed iron handle on stand. $155.00 up

TURNTABLE WAFFLE IRON
Embossed same both sides: WAGNER WARE, SIDNEY, O. 8 PAT'd Feb. 22,
1910; heavy wire bail on stand. $155.00 up

SPINNING BROILER
Imprinted: PATENT, ca. 1850; rare to find one as a casting since usually hand fashioned; unusual feature is the cup in the handle for catching juices, which were then spooned up to baste the meat. Could be English. $375.00 – $395.00 up

HANGING GRIDDLE
Found in Massachusetts. Ca. 1800; heavy bail, and legs so it can also be set on the hearth in the raked out coals; swivel ring for turning on the trammel hook or crane. $175.00 – $225.00

THREE STANDING (FOOTED GRIDDLES)
These are among the rarest forms of early American household cooking irons. Flat end handle: dated 1793. $395.00 – $425.00

Long handle eye, ca. 1850. $250.00

Round-eye handle; ca. 1810. $295.00 +

HOECAKE GRIDDLE (SKILLET) Imprinted: GRISWOLD MFG. CO. ERIE, PA. U.S.A. 1118; slightly deeper — bottom shown; 10½" dia.; grease-pouring lips. $75.00

GRIDDLE (SHALLOW SKILLET TYPE FOR OMELETS etc.) 10" diameter. Imprinted: WAGNER WARE, SIDNEY, O. #1098A; base shows imprinting; pouring-lips each side. $75.00 up

GRIDDLE for New England FIRECAKES (SHORTCAKES) ca. 1890s, 18"
diameter. $75.00

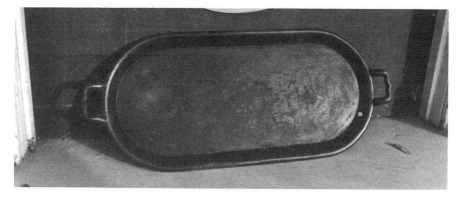

Family used this as a GRIDDLE; could also have been used as a broiler,
open baker, or for many cakes as at an inn. (Historical background plaque
indicates home was built in 1840.) $95.00

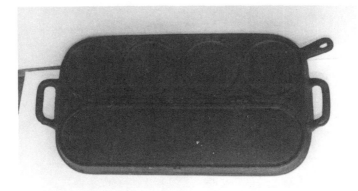

PANCAKES (HOTCAKES) IRON
For 4 cakes; when 1 side done can be flipped with handle onto other side to bake; also hanging and carrying handles. $85.00

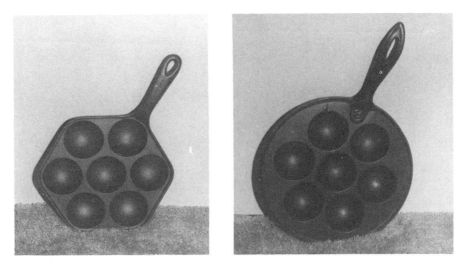

EGG FRYERS
Ca. 1890s. $85.00 each

GRIDDLE, HOTCAKES
Round; grooved handle.
$50.00

BACON and 2 EGGS SKIL-
LET. Wide handle. $50.00

IRON GRILLE
Embossed: RUSSELL'S
PAT. Apr. 9, 1867. 2 parts
hinged. $125.00

SALESMAN'S SAMPLE
MINIATURE GRIDDLE
Imprinted: WAGNER
WARE, SIDNEY, O.; heavy
wire bail; 4½" diameter.
$150.00

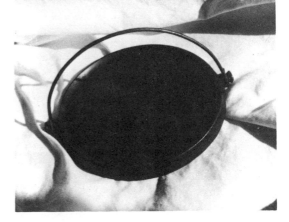

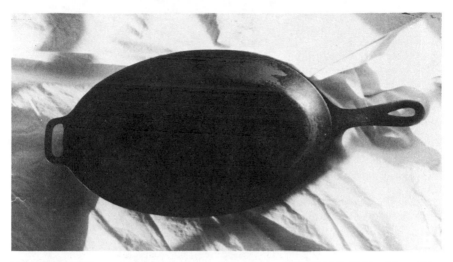

FISH SKILLET – a rarity. Imprinted on bottom: GRISWOLD MFG. CO., ERIE, PA., U.S.A. 2 handles for lifting and hanging. $175.00

FRY SKILLET Uncommon square one; GRISWOLD MFG. CO., ERIE, PA., U.S.A. #768 imprinted on bottom; 8½". $165.00

SPIDER
A frying pan on 3 legs for cooking over the hearth coals;
rat-tail handle. Ca. 1810 – 1820. $165.00 up

SKILLETS
Of various sizes, from 1850 into the early 1900s. $35.00 – $75.00

GRISSETS (RUSH DIP PANS) RARE CONTAINERS
Ca. 18th century; 1 Pennsylvania and the more worn New York origin. After its fat contents were melted over coals or hot ashes raked onto the hearth, rushes (as cattails) already peeled to their pith were soaked in the grease – or drawn slowly through – to heavily coat them; pressed together, they were hung to dry, later to be used for lighting in a rush holder. (More common was an oblong bowl-shaped ladle which soaked the rushes in hot fat – or even poured the fat over them.) Grissets were usually found in England, beginning in usage during the 15th century, but these are American. $450.00 – $525.00 each

GYPSY KETTLE BULBOUS TYPE
Short flat bar fingergrip; 3 stubby feet; original heavy wire bail. $100.00;
BEAN POT; Maker: BLUE VALLEY CO. KANSAS CITY, MO.: Ca. 1920s;
good-size thimble finial; 3 stubby feet; unusual item. $145.00

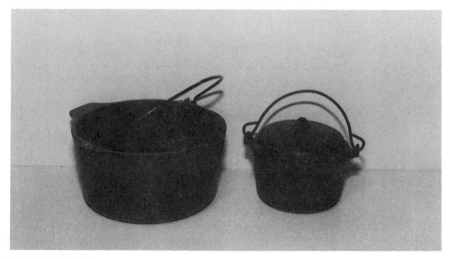

OPEN KETTLE
Imprinted: GRISWOLD, ERIE, PA. Pouring lip; tip bar and ring; heavy wire
bail. $55.00; (Smallest) BAKER; domed lid with small fingergrip bar;
imprinted: P & B Pattern #190; a rarity. $150.00

BAKER with self-steaming lid that "drips," lid has a heavy handle; a useful inherited item; "6" for 6 Qts. $75.00

COOKING POT with 3 feet; heavy bail; pouring lip and tipping ear pulled from casting; ca. 1880's bulged round bottom. $55.00

SCOTCH BOWL
Ca. 1890; sloping sides; heavy wire bail, tipping ring 1 side under bar; had no lid because cracked wheat porridges, thick Scotch barley soups, and such foods needed constant stirring while being cooked so they would not stick to the pan. $95.00 up

POTATO BAKER
In 3 parts with liftout grille for cleaning; all original; tipping ring low front base of kettle. $75.00

Bulge bottom SKILLET or rat-tail handled PAN. Early. $275.00 up

OPEN COOKING POT with sharp ears; 3 stubby feet and wrought bail; unique piece. Early. $250.00 up

SCOTCH TYPE OPEN BOWL POT
New bail; tiny thimble ears each side between bail-rings indicate it could fit into a cradle over the fire as well as hang from a crane, trammel, or chainhooks. Ca. 1800s. $145.00 and more according to area

DEEP KETTLE
Tiny ears could rest on a cradle; new bail size indicates it could have been used for small amounts of applebutter, big family stews, or cornmeal mush which boils into big bubbles that plop and splatter; could also be hung from a trammel. $145.00 +

OPEN COOKING POT
Interesting ears holding
heavy wire bail. Ca. 1800s.
$145.00 up

**GYPSY KETTLE (COOKING
POT)**
9" high x 10½" diameter; 3
short legs; heavy iron wire
bail; ca. 1800s; bulbous.
These are seldom marked.
They must have been stan-
dard items with most
foundries for there were so
many around until recent-
ly; now they take a bit of
looking; widely repro-
duced. $95.00 up for one in
good condition.

WASHBOILER
2 handle bars and 4 short legs; an essential of every home was a vessel that could hold a large amount of water to be heated. $45.00

BAKER
with handled lid; bail; raised self-drip bars inside lid. $45.00 +

DOUBLE BOILER
Ca. 1850 – 1860. 16" high x 13" diameter; removable wire basket hung by hook at center of bail; all original. $125.00 complete

HILL'S CHAMPION STEAM COOKER #10 Embossed: HILL WHITNEY & CO., BOSTON, MASS. Ptd. Aug. 16, 1887; 2 pcs., top grooved to fit into bottom. Set over the cooking stove well; water in the base forced steam through the tube, cooking food in the lidded sheet tin top; cast iron bail, wood handlegrip. $125.00 variable complete

OUTDOOR KETTLE Embossed: COOK "N" KETTLE. 3 pcs. with heavy wire bail; liftout inside grid; Trade Mark: REGISTERED COOK "N" TOOLS, INC., TULSA, OKLA.; 3 small feet; slide top ventilator; note twisted wire grip; (shown on stand as used by owners.) $125.00

Unusual cast iron BOWL (Shaped similar to an early trencher), ca. early 1800s. $135.00 variable

CAST HANDLE FOOD-CHOPPER With double tang heavy rolled sheet tin blades; embossed: NRS & CO. GROTON, N.Y. PATd. May 2, 1893 No. 20. $95.00

FIREFENDER (KERB)
24" long x 5" high x 6" deep; overall patterned. $175.00 up

FIREBACK
Very early; ornate overall patterns with roses, beading, an urn of flowers, and pineapples, our colonial emblem of hospitality; very heavy as were all quality old fireplace accessories. $295.00 up

FIREBACK
Colonial Lady riding sidesaddle on a prancing horse, medallion, floral border; (andirons are wrought). $425.00

ANDIRONS
15½" high; can hold big logs; polished; cast and wrought. $150.00 – $225.00 up pr.

ANDIRONS
16" high. $210.00 pair

Cast **FIREFRONT** with hand-hammered finish combined with fancy
FIREFENDER having inverted acorn finials. On front are 2 phoenix birds,
urn, and scrolls. Penn. origin. 23" high x 25" wide. $350.00+ set

GRATE BASKET
$85.00

FIREPLACE FRONTS (Covers)
Uncommon to find a pair; 30" high x 26½" wide each; protection at night and in family's absence against live coals exploding out onto the floor; Victorians enjoyed them to hide silent fireplace during summer months, sometimes putting a pot of ferns in front of the iron; 2 pcs. each, fronts and frames. $250.00 each 2 part section; $500.00 complete pair and more to area.

FIREFRONT
2 Pcs. 30" high x 28" wide; handsomely ornate. $310.00 up

SNOWBIRDS
Fastened to roofs with their long iron rods to (hopefully) prevent snow sliding off onto heads of passersby; others felt the snow helped hold heat beneath; began as cast bird forms, then expanded to many patterns, but thus the name. Ca. 1800s. $55.00 each

PITCHER PUMP
(It is not always advisable to change the appearances or original usages of fine old items, but here the original form remains, converted by the addition of unobtrusive parts into a lamp.) Lamp only 10" high x 8" wide with nose; original red color; and the base is cut from an old barn beam. (C.T. Cat is only a curious onlooker.) Pump Value Only: $95.00

PITCHER PUMP
Embossed: RED JACKET MFG. CO. DAVENPORT, IOWA NO. 1A This company produced many pumps in various models and sizes. $75.00 variable

FORCE PUMP #201
For outside usage usually; widest part of base cutout crisscross pattern; bucket bail hung on spur; three lower pipes inserted into the well or cistern; maker embossed: MAST FOOS & COMPANY SPRINGFIELD, OHIO. $125.00

ICE TONGS
$38.00

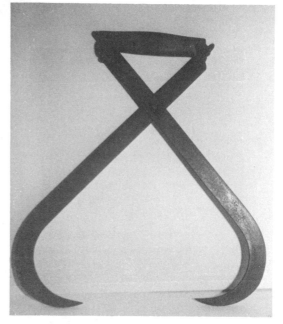

120

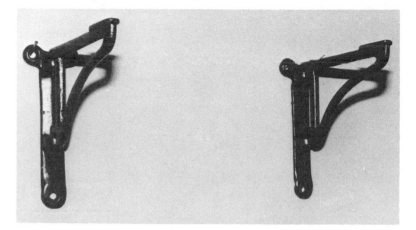

**Side-turning SHELF BRACKETS. Original finish; 2 parts; 5½" high.
$40.00 pair**

HOUSEHOLD SPICE MILL
Wood base, drawer front,
and handlegrip; side
adjustable screw; could
also get a coarse grind if
using for cornmeal, grits,
etc. $225.00 +

HOUSEHOLD COFFEE GRINDER Embossed: LANDERS FRARY & CLARK NEW BRITAIN, CONN.; late 1800s (could also have been size used by a small crossroads store). $550.00 – $575.00 up variable

COFFEE GRINDERS (MILLS)
Two sizes with important cast iron parts; inside grinders crushed the beans. $95.00 each variable

COFFEE GRINDER
Cast iron and wood; ornately embossed top has 2 sliding panels that open for beans to be poured inside where the wheel grinds them, and ground coffee drops into drawer at bottom. $125.00

COFFEE GRINDER
Wall mounted; TRADE-MARK: #11 STEINFELD; beans in glass jar at top drop onto grinding wheel inside, activated by manually turning the handle; ground coffee drops into a (missing) glass tumbler or tin cup set on the cutout design base; ca.: 1910. $75.00 up

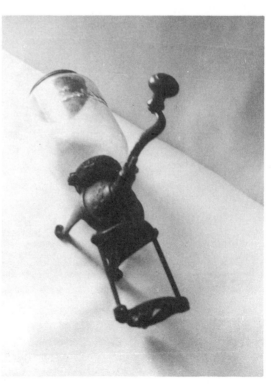

BASE ONLY COFFEE GRINDER to show skillful pattern used for this casting; embossed: ARCADE – CRYSTAL; gilt painted; glass top (missing) was originally as with Steinfeld Model; glass or cup set below to catch ground coffee; ca. 1890 – 1910. $48.00 as is

Left: TURNTABLE APPLE PARER (smallest of the three). Embossed: Manfd. BY LOCKEY & HOWLAND; Patented June 17 and Dec. 16, 1856. $65.00
Center: COFFEE GRINDER. Embossed: LANDERS, FRARY & CLARK NEW BRITAIN, CONN. Patd. Aug. 31, 1909 and Feb. 14, 1905. $65.00
Right: CHERRY STONER (SEEDER). PAT'D Mar. 31, 1903; ENTERPRISE MFG. CO., PHILA. PA. $68.00+

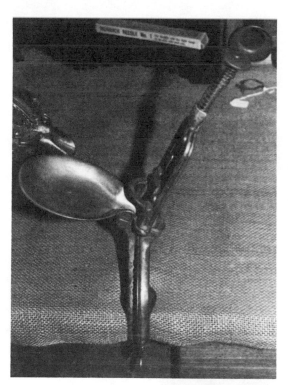

CHERRY STONER
Top spring action; New Standard, Mount Joy, Pa., ca. 1900. $65.00

CHERRY STONER (PITTER)
3 wrought legs; operable; embossed: PATd. Nov. 17, 1863. $95.00 up

CHERRY STONER (PITTER)
Pat. Dtd. Nov. 17, 1863 and May 15, 1866; 4 legs; turn-handle. $125.00 +

APPLE PARER
Embossed: READING HARDWARE CO. READING, PA. PATd. March 5, 1872; side turn-handle; apple held by 3-pronged spit. $55.00

APPLE PARER
Embossed: MADE
ONLY BY THE READ-
ING HARDWARE CO.
READING, PA. PATd.
May 5, 1868 – 1875 –
1877; fully operable.
(Screw at base miss-
ing.) $55.00

EGG SCALE
Farm used; 8½" high x
6½" wide x 3" deep; 3 brief
feet; red weighing arm;
wrought spike; aluminum
weight indicator; brass
head screw levels scale.
$48.00

NUTCRACKER
Embossed: PERFECTION
NUT CRACKER Patented;
on opposite side: Malleable Iron Fitting Co,
Branford, Conn. $48.00

DOG NUTCRACKER ON BASE
Depressing tail causes lower jaw to crack the shell against the upper jaw;
all original; carefully cast design. (Found at former Murfreesboro, Tenn.
Cedar Bucket Factory.) $125.00. SQUIRREL NUTCRACKER is new. Same
principle applied as on the old. Sold as new @ $10.00. An original would be
valued about $45.00 up.

DOG NUTCRACKER ON PLAIN BASE
Embossed: HARPERS SUPPLY CO. CHICAGO – Pat. Appld. For. Source embossing on its base increases the value. $125.00

LEMON SQUEEZERS
Each has 2 jointed parts; all original. Taller standing embossed: TOWNSEND LEMON SQUEEZER PHILADELPHIA, PATd. May 30, 1866. $75.00 Smaller standing embossed: PEARL. $55.00 Lying flat on table: white ironstone center holder; Pat. 1868. $125.00

NUTCRACKER
Ca. 1895 – 1900; 2 jointed handles are opened and closed to crack shells of nuts lying in the open ring between them. $35.00
MODERN ICE SHAVER, ca. mid-1900s. Embossed: ARCTIC ICE SHAVE #33 Grey Iron Casting Co., Mount Joy, Pa. U.S.A. $35.00
Seen among Pantry Collectibles in a shop as one of the upcoming "savables."

DOORSTOP
Once known as a DOOR PORTER; from the 1700s they were made from glass, pottery, even wood; iron castings were popular here after the Civil War; usage was to hold doors open for ventilation.
POT of THISTLES on a base; uncommon to find this pattern; ca. 1860. $195.00 – $225.00

DOORSTOP
Flower basket with a handle bow. $275.00 – 350.00

DOORSTOP
All original graceful COR-NUCOPIA of FLOWERS on a base; note how it is offset at the bottom to balance blossoms, a thoughtful patternmaker; ca. last half 1800s; uncommon. $350.00

DOORSTOP
Ship; patterns often copied from styles of early French vessels and Spanish galleons; original colors. $250.00 up

DOORSTOP
Ship in full sail; original colors. $250.00 up

DOORSTOP
(Thought to represent flagship of Columbus — the Santa Maria), ca. 1880 – 1890; original in the off-white and related soft colors. $245.00 up

DOORSTOP
Ship with the iron hoop for easier handling; painted black over its original pastel, so the value is reduced. $125.00

DOORSTOP
PRAIRIE SCHOONER; original colors; ca. 1860s. $250.00 up

DOOR PORTER (STOP)
These were so ornamental in their original lovely colors they surely must have been sometimes set at the hearth as decorative at that focal point of the home. Spanish- or French-influenced Ship in full sail. $250.00 up

DOORSTOP
Called the BLUE HOUSE from its original coloring. $185.00

DUCK
Solid metal with casting seam down the back; good wear on original natural colors; from a skillful patternmaker; ca. 1870 – 1880. $425.00

A SNAKE – A RATTLER!!!
Realistic original paint on this diamondback; rattles easily visible at the end of the tail; ca. 1880. $435.00

The original CAT
DOORSTOP. $195.00 +

The COPIED CAT
DOORSTOP, 1978; still
being made; differences in
expression easily visible,
position of head; overall
10¾" high; sold as NEW.
$45.00

PARROT type BIRD DOOR STOP 8¼" high; good original colors. $295.00 – $325.00

DOORSTOPS
Gilded Elephant, very heavy though small. $135.00
Gilded Lion. $155.00

DOORSTOP
Reproduced FOX and
BOOTS, ca. 1949. $65.00

DOORSTOP, WIRE HAIR TERRIER
Small but heavy; ca. 1900. $175.00
COCKER SPANIEL
1 side only casting but heavy enough to hold open a door. $250.00 without collar
chain

DOORSTOPS
Regal Siamese CAT. $120.00; SCOTTISH TERRIERS. $225.00

DOORSTOPS
BOSTON TERRIER. $150.00 no collar; ENGLISH SETTER, original colors.
$195.00 – $225.00

DOORSTOPS, BOSTON TERRIERS
original colors. $195.00 – $275.00 each with collars

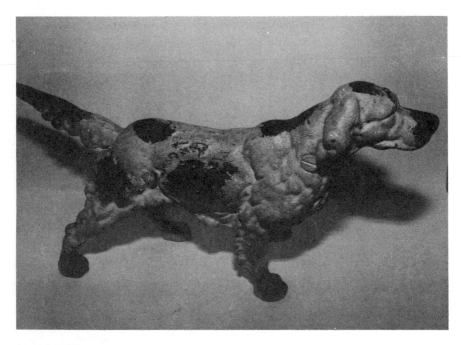

DOORSTOP, ENGLISH SETTER
7½" high; original colors. $195.00 – $225.00

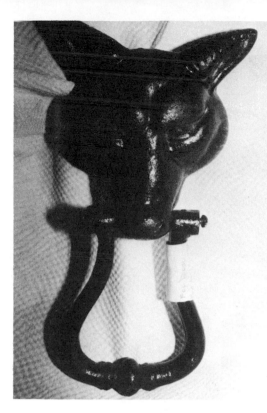

DOORKNOCKER
As conveniences to visitors, they have been used since our Pilgrim times; FOX'S HEAD with ring in mouth; 5½" high head; expert patternmaking noted in expressive eyes and ears. $145.00 +

DOORKNOCKERS
Flowerbasket knocker resounding against openwork patterned plate; original colors. $125.00
Owl; also is clapped against rim-grooved plate; original colors. $145.00

CLAW FOOT
(Good paperweight without changing the original structure) 6½" long; holding solid glass ball; probably a piece from a large Victorian parlor table. Once found at most market places; now scarce. $75.00

BOOKENDS
These are fast gaining popularity as a collectible; a design of farmhouse, trees, and bridge over a stream; original good colors. $125.00 pair

BOOKENDS
Painted black at some time through the years since they were originally in pastels. $65.00 pair. Value at least $25.00 each, priced higher if still in original colors.

MATCHBOX
Held woodstick, sulphur-tipped "kitchen" matches; depressing the side base lever allowed matches inside to drop onto lower tray; Pat. dates October 29, May 11, December 2, all 1897. $155.00

MATCHBOX
Elaborately cast; open tray to reach in for sulphur "kitchen" matches; hung on wall. $68.00

MATCHHOLDER
Fly whose wings can be lifted for storage of sulphur matches in body "box." $125.00

MATCHHOLDER
High-button Shoe holds long sulphur matches; ca. 1890s. Many copies seen. $55.00

MATCHBOX
Wall hanger; Antlered Stag; iron knobbed door opens for matches stored inside box. $125.00 +

TOYS

Toy castings reached their peak by the late 1800's, continuing as far as the 1940's although to a lesser degree. Locomotives with cars and horse-drawn vehicles were particularly well liked in the 1880's. It is sometimes difficult to detect cast iron reproductions but many of the original old makers embossed or at least imprinted their names. This is not typical of modern copies. Look for natural wear and dimming of original colors, since both are difficult to successfully reproduce. Old colors are susceptible to chipping and scratching. And, again, intricate and expressive details can be smoothed down or altogether ignored. With the urgent need for all metals during World War II, "unessential" castings ceased. (Someone once told me that a deliberate copy of the old is a compliment to the original – but at parallel prices it does seem to be a costly purchasing error.)

FIRE ENGINE PUMPER with FIREMAN
ca. 1890; original paint on black horses, red wagon, yellow wheels. $400.00 – $450.00 and variable +

PONY CART (SULKY) with DRIVER
8" wide, ca. 1897. (Reins missing) $325.00

HORSE with LUMBER CART
Handsomely-cast horse; 2-wheeled vehicle; ca. 1850 – 1860.
$350.00 +

GOAT WAGON EXPRESS WITH DRIVER
Original colors dimmed; ca. 1900 to 1920s. $415.00 up

FLOOR TRAIN
Not equipped with tracks or wheel construction to fit them; children pulled or pushed along the floors; ca. 1870; note mixed passenger and freight cars; L&N RR. $275.00 up more to area

FLOOR TRAIN
Engine, tender, and passenger coach showing seats through the windows; ERIE RR Engine #400; 1800s. $295.00 up more to area

LOCOMOTIVE
Original red and black paint; floor toy. $225.00 +

MODEL T COUPE
$295.00 – $325.00

ROW of STOVES
From early coal and wood cookstoves to the top center white gas burner with two side ovens, one of which is a warming oven and broiler, prices variable beginning at a minimum of $155.00 – $250.00 +

TOY STOVE, embossed on front: EAGLE; nickel-plated; complete; has old toy cooking pot and lidlifter, maker: L.J. BROMERS MFG. CO. $350.00 + set of 3 pieces PUPPY PAPERWEIGHT on floor. $45.00

TOY COOKSTOVE, STAR on front and side shelf, stars "touched up." Owner made new stovepipe similar to the original design. $175.00

TOY STOVE
Embossed on oven door: ACME; 12" high x 13½" deep; complete as original; with lidlifter. $395.00 +

TOY STOVE
Embossed ACME on front oven door; restored stovepipe, curved shelves and top. With lidlifter. $375.00 up

CANNON
Early; 15" wide x 5" high; depressing finger lever at top rear of
platform activates paper caps. $225.00 min.

ROWS of CANNONS
Ca. 1800s; various sizes, styles, values. $225.00 min. – $450.00 variable

BANKS

Banks of some form and material have existed for over 2000 years. Whether called Penny, Piggy, or Coin Banks, they appeared when coin currency appeared. Archaeologists have found them among the artifacts of early civilizations, from little square boxes to more elaborate forms. Pigs were once regarded as symbols of good luck, and the saying "keep the wolf from the door" stresses thrift.

MECHANICAL BANKS are those where movement begins as a coin is deposited; REGISTERING BANKS, never popular, operate as Cash Registers, automatically adding totals as coins are put in (sometimes one pulls a lever); and STILL BANKS, most popular of all, less expensive and always in heavier production, merely retained deposits without mechanical movement. All are intended to teach "saving for a rainy day." There were silver and gilt finishes; others were electroplated with nickel (as some toy stoves) or copper, and still others were treated with what the makers termed "aluminum or gold bronze."

TAMMANY
PAT'd. December 23, 1873 and June 8, 1875; a coin placed in the right hand is deposited in his coat pocket as he nods his thanks; original colors in gray pants, black jacket, yellow vest; 5¾" high; embossed at side: TAMMANY BANK. This bank represents the notorious Boss Tweed during New York City political irregularities in the early 1870s; Tammany was heavily produced by J.E. STEVENS & CO. When the scandals abated, the bank's name was changed to "FAT MAN"; still operable. Very good original paint $2,000.00, medium $750.00 up

HUMPTY DUMPTY
7" high; in the 1800s pantomimist George Washington Fox created the character for whom this bank was named; pressing a lever behind his left shoulder lIfts the arm and hand holding the coin, drops the coin into the mouth as the eyes roll; embossed maker: SHEPARD HARDWARE MFG. CO. BUFFALO, N.Y.: PATd. March 14, 1882, June 17, 1884; operable. $900.00; if mint version, $1,000.00 up

JOLLY
6¾" high; the only one American-made although there are other busts; Patent date November 14, 1882 is always embossed on the back of originals along with the maker: SHEPARD HARDWARE CO. first and later by J. E. STEVENS CO., CROMWELL, CONN.; wearing a red shirt. Excellent condition. Begins at $1,000.00.

KICKING (MILKING) COW
5½" high x 9¾" wide x 3½" deep; operable; green base; coin deposited in slot on cow's back, flower-tipped lever at animal's front controlled by spring at left rear hoof causes her to swish her tail, and kick up her rear leg, dumping milker off his stool with contents of pail flipped into his face; he is manually set back in place as his feet hinge in the base; traces of red paint on fence; ca. 1888; mfgd. by J.E. STEVENS & CO., CROMWELL, CONN; all original. $2,500.00 – $3,000.00 up

ARTILLERY BANK (one of the most heavily reproduced mechanicals) 6½" high x 8¾" wide; 4-sided blockhouse, 8-sided a rarity; operable; coin placed inside on cannon's half-shelf flies over into the blockhouse as lever at back trips spring; soldier's raised arm comes down; red, white, blue uniform; imprinted: PAT'd. 1875 – 1897. Minimum $1,000.00 to $2,100.00 much more to area.

ELEPHANT
2 parts held with side screw; depressing the tail activates spring, causing coin placed in trunk to be raised and deposited in slot at the head; ca. early 1900s. $975.00 up to area There are several mechanical elephant types. The older ROYAL ELEPHANT drops a coin into a richly cast seat (oriental howdah) high on its back; its value is considerably higher. $1,050.00 up

Most originals are tightly joined together, have sharp well-defined details, and are smooth to the touch. Those in good condition are of course most valuable. Stills were cast in foundries, as the mechanicals, although most of the stills were more simply cast in 2 parts for joining, or the roof comprising a 3rd part. Many manufacturers produced innumerable buildings in many styles and sizes, the larger being more scarce and more expensive. Since the old paints did chip and scar, it is best not to repaint or "touch up" as it impairs the value; reproductions can be less carefully put together and finishes can be overly bright, lacking the lovely patina of age and handling.

INDEPENDENCE HALL
10½" high x 9½" wide x 5" deep; embossed: BIRTH-PLACE OF AMERICAN INDEPENDENCE, Patd. September 14, 1875; also embossed: ENTERPRISE MFG. CO., PHILA. (Clock is set at 3:26.) $1,800.00 – $3,000.00

WOOLWORTH BUILDING
7¾" high x 2¼" deep x 1½" wide; note detailed windows; this in New York City is among the desired building collectibles. $175.00

VICTORIAN RESIDENCE
Again the variety of size and design, confusing to collectors; original paint good; 5" high x 3" wide x 2¼" deep. $175.00

BANK BUILDING
Embossed: 1882 above the doors; 5½" high x 3¾" wide x 2¾" deep; roof separately held by chimney-end of long bolt in turn fastened into base, making it a 3-part casting; coin deposit in roof. Many makers produced banks, among them KENTON HARDWARE CO., KENTON, O. and Chicago's WING MANUFACTURING COMPANY. $275.00

YELLOW BANK BUILDING
5¼" high x 3½" wide x 2½" deep; attractive cutouts. $150.00 up

TOWER BANK BUILDING
3¾" high x 1½" deep x 2½" long; ca. 1890. $225.00 up

TAJ MAHAL
Ca. 1880; 4½" high x 3½" wide x 2½" deep; front view with coin slot, back with screw joiner; entirely original. (Shah Jahan, ruler of Agra, a province in Northern India, built this tomb for his beloved favorite wife, Mumtaz-i-Mahal. The Taj Mahal was built between 1632 and 1653 and is considered one of the most beautiful building $275.00 – $325.00

BILLIKEN
4¼" high x 2½" wide x 2½" deep; gold (bronze) finish with traces of original red pants and blue jacket; mfgd. by A.C. WILLIAMS CO., RAVENNA, O., Pattern imprinted: 3960 – with GOOD LUCK on the back. Billiken was copied from a grotesque doll about 1905 and thought by some to bring good fortune. $200.00 – $300.00

BANK BUILDING
4½" high x 2" deep x 3¼" wide; Embossed: BANK above slot and screw fastener. 3 parts. $195.00 variable to area.

INDIAN CHIEF
6" high, with war bonnet and holding tomahawk; claw necklace; finely-patterned face with stern expression, hand shading eyes as he peers into the distance; traces of original colors; stands on moccasined feet unsupported; coin slot and screw at back. $650.00 + up to area

157

ROWS OF BANKS
Many sizes, styles, and decorating themes of SECURITY SAFE DEPOSIT BANKS, Key and Combination locks; prices are variable from a minimum $100.00 to many hundreds, each dependent upon embossed or imprinted maker's names, dates, or marks, since these are in fine condition. Among them is a large SAFE, with 1 deep and 2 smaller security drawers inside – minimum $500.00. Another is the silvered combination lock SAFE showing an embossed blacksmith with his hammer in his hand and other tools lying about, minimum $500.00

SECURITY DEPOSIT SAFE BANK
Safe banks were ordinarily copied after actual full-size working ones in business establishments; 3¾" wide x 4¼" x 6" high; wide bar handles each side; combination to "8". $600.00 up
SAFE BANK
Combination to "8" on dial; double doors unusual; 6¼ wide x 5¾" high x 4" deep; designs appropriate to large shield on one door repeated at top, sides, and corners; ca. 1870 – 1880. $600.00

SAFE DEPOSIT
Imprinted on base: patd. August 24, 1897; leaf and star patterns; 3" wide x 2½" deep x 4" high. $250.00 up
SAFE BANK
Combination; heavily pattern embossed; column-corners. $600.00 up
SECURITY SAFE
Berry, acorn, and fruit design; ornate combination elaborate double star embossed: A F; imprinted on bottom: PAT. FEB. 11, 81, March 1, 87; 3" wide x 3" deep x 4¼" high. $400.00 – $600.00

CHERUB SAFE
Combination to "9"; gilt on front and 4 side; 4¼" wide x 6" high x 3½" deep; cherub with wings decor; retractable handle; ca. 1890. $650.00 +

COLUMBUS SAFE
So embossed with a large center STAR; urns each side, petalled star on top; 4¼" wide x 4" deep x 5¼" high; combination to "9". $325.00
BURGLAR-PROOF HOUSE SAFE at center
So embossed; combination to "8" in an uncommonly detailed circle of flower petals; retractable handle; 4¾" wide x 4⅛" deep x 5¾" high; horns of plenty, urns, scrolls, and flowers on front, sides, and top; ca. 1880s. $350.00 up
THE HOME SAVINGS BANK
4" wide x 3½" deep x 5⅜" high; Top has: Savings Deposit inside and a laurel wreath; combination to "9". $325.00 up

SAFE BANK
Key opener; 4½" wide x 6½" high x 3¾" deep; dull and bright finish; flower design; retractable handle. $275.00 up

SAFE BANK
Gilt front; heavily embossed designs, top has 2 winged cherubim; retractable handle; combination; 4¼" wide x 3½" deep x 6" high. $400.00 – $500.00 up

DAISY SAFE
Tin sides and back; desirable; 2¾" wide x 2¾" deep x 3½ high; key. $195.00 up

LARGE ARABIAN SAFE
3¾" wide x 3½" deep x 5" high, Key, decorated with desert scenes. $500.00 – $600.00 up

SAFE BANK
GARGOYLE AND SCROLL, tin sides and back; bottom embossed: KENTON; 3¼" wide x 3" deep x 4¼" high; combination. $375.00 – $400.00 up

STATE SAFE
2 sides tin – 2⅞" wide x 2⅞" deep x 3⅛" high; combination opened. (Tin banks were made by traveling tinners creating primitive little box shapes from materials scraps, small tabs bent to open and close soon broke off.) Highly collectible; commercially successful by the 1860s. $195.00 up
SAFE BANK
Key; original green and yellow paint; 4-leaf clover cutouts; 2¼" wide x 2⅛" deep x 3⅜" high; 4 sides cutout design; imprinted on base: PTD. APPLD. FOR. $195.00
SAFE BANK
Combination; embossed on front: J.W. LONG CLOTHIER, THE BOYS' BEST FRIEND, LAKE GENEVA; imprinted on bottom: REGENT MFG. CO. Chicago; 2⅝" wide x 2⅝" deep x 4" high; dog with winged cherub blowing a trumpet on sides and embossed on the back a seated child and dog. $400.00 – $500.00 up

Key COIN BANK
4¾" wide x 2¾" deep x 4" high; retractable handle; ornately cast with floral panels and peacock eye borders. $750.00 up
Combination COIN BANK
Embossed: PATENT PENDING 1905 Jewel-like studded door panel, ornate. $500.00 up

ANIMAL STILL BANKS
TURKEY. $175.00
COW, 3½" high, paint good. $145.00
HORSE on TUB, mint condition. $200.00
MULE, good color. $175.00

LION
5½" long x 4" high; silver gilt finished; these made in many sizes and positions. $160.00 variable
ELEPHANT ON TUB
Silver gilt finish (some were painted, others electroplated with nickel or copper, and still others with what makers termed "aluminum or gold bronze"); red tub, saddle with moon and stars. And the tusks are intact! $230.00 variable

OTHERS – PLAIN and FANCY

URN
Set on cast iron base; 36"
high; maker: GRAY & DUD-
LEY, PHILA. ca. 1860 –
1870. $1,250.00 – $1,300.00

**URN ca. mid-1800s; 30"
high, 24" top diameter;
ornate; once at Stella Niagara on the Niagara Fron-
tier. Owner declared it
"priceless." $1,800.00 up**

FRUIT BOWL, Victorian; low pedestal; lacy design of flowers, leaves, and acorns; 1" wide basketweave rim; overall diameter 11", 2" high. $145.00

PLATE
Gothic design, cast iron washed with copper and then lightly silvered, now almost entirely worn off; 7¾" diameter, 1½" wide rim with blackberry design and square cut edge; heavy. $175.00 – $195.00

STOVEBACK PIECE WINGED LIONS
5¼" high x 11½" wide; long since detached, they remain lovely today.
$195.00 +

ORNAMENTAL TRIM
Lost long ago from a horse-drawn carriage; ca. 1800s. $65.00

**GRATING or GRILLE
WORK COVER**
Ca. 1870; lavishly
designed; 10½" high x
7½" wide; 3 screw holes.
$315.00 – $325.00

**PARTS from decorative VENT COVERS or GRILLE WORK once on a home
built about 1860. $15.00 – $18.00**

HOOKS
$45.00 + each

INCENSE BURNER
Owl's Head, 2 pcs., very old.
$95.00

**CANDLESTICK, gargoyle,
leaves, and berries; 9" high;
ca. mid-1800s. $150.00 +**

DOUBLE CANDLESTICK
(wIthout candles); 12" high.
$75.00

STATUARY, Harpooner in Boat (harpoon missing); used on a stair's newel post; electrified at a later date from original ca. 1800; colors still good. $175.00

BALL once atop a water tank in a northern N.Y. state village; (this type of item sought for business foyers and the like). 21" high x 14" diameter. $225.00

FENCE SPEARS
(atop laced wire) fence sections $125.00 – $150.00. If spears were removed and sold individually, about $75.00 each up

GATE and FENCING with acorn finials on posts; values greatly varied to section of country.

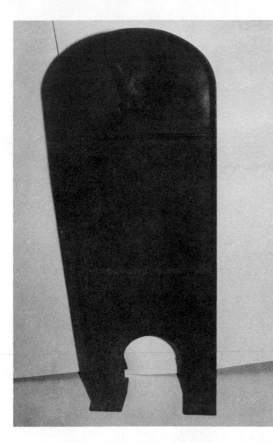

CEMETERY MARKER (HEADSTONE)
RARE to find in cast iron; embossed around curved center base: Pat. March 22, 1887; leaf cluster above that; a dove in flight on the top panel; inscription panel space at center; never installed. $225.00 up

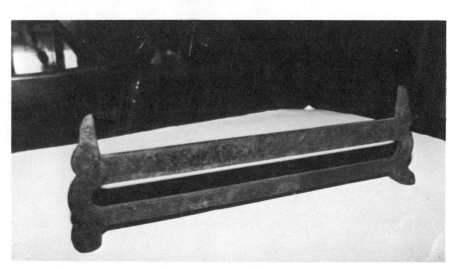

The PLAIN BOOTSCRAPER
Embossed: P&C DARAIN #33. $45.00

THE COPY of a popular style of MUDSCRAPER ornately cast over old pattern. 9" high x 11" wide. $75.00 – $95.00

The FANCY BOOTJACK Embossed: TRY ME (style typical of Strause Gas Iron Co., Philadelphia). $95.00

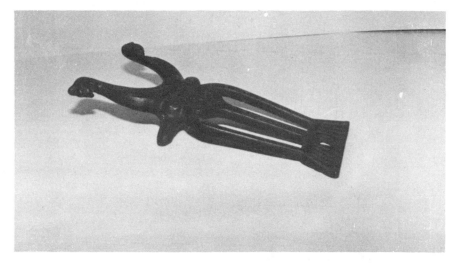

BOOTJACK
Beetle shaped jaws; sometimes called just "beetles" because they resemble the shape of the insect; several styles made; ca. 1880. $115.00

For decorating the mantels' hearthsides, these pieces were enjoyed in the 1700s; after our 1800s Industrial Revolution, a greater number of people could purchase them. They could be seen largely in kitchens, the gathering places of earlier homes. Parlors were saved for entertaining the preacher and the more formal visitors. Popular patterns were animals, birds, houses, country couples leaning against fence gates. Produced in small workshops, the supply was understandably limited, and the larger foundries didn't wish to make them when standard quantity production items had become so much more profitable. Few such pieces remain.

HORSES
All original; one 8" high x 8½" in length; one 7½" high x 10½" in length; ca. 1800s. $195.00 + each

ELEPHANT
Holding water cup aloft; held to base by screw. $110.00 – $125.00

174

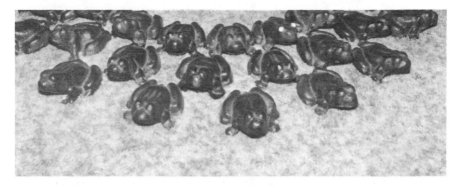

COLLECTION OF BULLFROG DOORSTOPS (note detailed work)
The only one not cast iron is brass, the one with the white eyes. All late
1800s to early 1900s. Iron, $135.00 – $165.00 each. (The brass, $195.00 +)

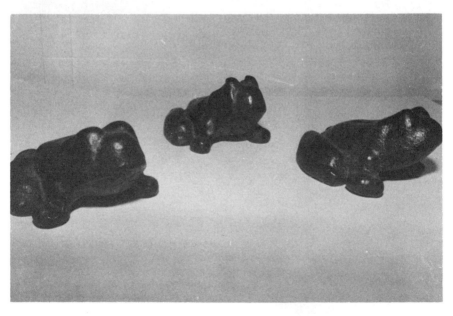

FROGS
Ca. late 1800s, early 1900s. Could be ORNAMENTS set at the hearth or
HEAVY DOORSTOPS; my grandmother had one that always sat back of the
parlor door, deceptively realistic with its time-worn dark green and brown
blending colors; these look ready to croak. $165.00 each (Very large ones
up to $500.00 each.)

Original HORSEHEAD once on a fluted post for complete HITCHING POSTS, 1800s; note fine casting of deeply hooded eyes, muzzle indentations, the thick, well-defined lips (not so emphasized on reproductions), carefully shaped ears, and the deep lines alongside the jaw, all giving expression; the ring is larger than on originals. Head only, $175.00 – $200.00; With an original post, $250.00 – $350.00 up

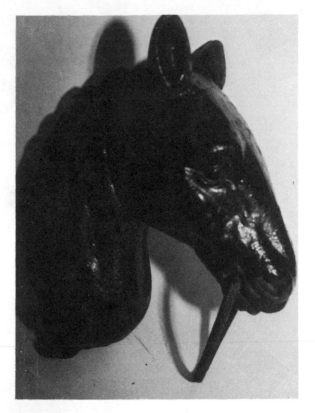

COPY of HORSE'S HEAD on post; albeit attractive in its sylvan setting, the expression is bland, details flattened compared to original, (as with new pressed glass copying the old). $65.00 up

CHURCH BELL
24" diameter, all original with large clapper; embossed: C.S. BELL & CO., HILLSBORO, O., (they specialized in big bells); ca. turn of our century; shown on new wood display stand. $1,200.00 – $1,350.00

BOXING (BOUTS) BELL (as called by Canadian dealer)
8" diameter, original paper stamp of supplier, SAFETY SUPPLY CO., TORONTO; embossed maker: BEVIN. $225.00 +

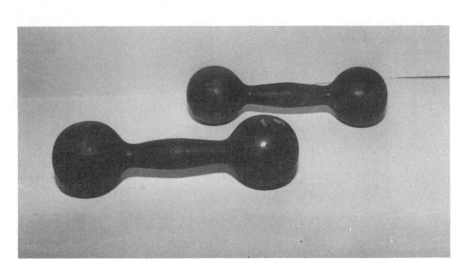

DUMBBELLS
4lbs; ca. 1880. $65.00 pair

DUMBBELLS
60 lbs. each; ca. 1870. $95.00 pair

HOOK, 17" long with 4 stubby drags, seen in western N.Y. $42.50

FIRE HYDRANT, complete; embossed: MUELLER CO., CHATTANOOGA, TENN. PATd. This one was marked Not for Sale but included here as important Americana. For others, prices variable from $225.00 up

Sides and front view of a RAILROAD STEAM LOCO-MOTIVE HEAD LAMP dated 1890; embossed: GOLDEN GLOW, ESSCO, PHILA. EUGENE #1; 19" across, 22" long, all original with glass unbroken; heavy. $675.00 up

BOAT ANCHOR
14" long x 8" wide;
embossed: KAUKAUNA,
WIS, M16; heavy flukes.
$75.00

SHIP'S ANCHOR
Found in the Gulf of
Mexico off Pensaco-
la, Florida. Barnacles
can form in as little
as a week so are no
true indication that
piece has been long
submerged. Early
Greeks accredited
with having the first
iron anchors. Value
varies according to
area and demand.

RAILROAD TRACK MEA-SURING GAUGE
Overall 60" long; New York Central lines; wood handle portion between cast tool ends. $75.00 up

PICK AXE used on New York Central lines; 36" with wood handle. $75.00 up

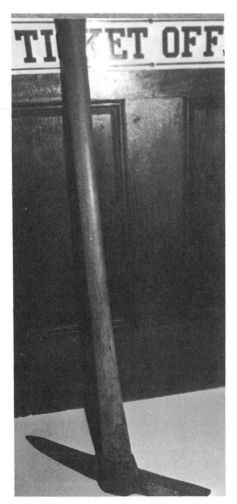

CAST IRON FITTINGS on a New York Central BAGGAGE WAGON hand pulled; no information available on iron object lying there. $300.00 variable

MAILBOX
Embossed: PAT'd. June 8, 1900 and LETTERS. From a small Nebraska town; first red-painted, later blue; taken out of active usage about 50 years ago. $195.00 +

MAST LANTERN from old Erie Canal Barge, found in Lockport, N.Y., scene of the old locks; complete; embossed: DRESSEL, ARLINGTON, N.J. U.S.A., the maker; also: MOHAWK LAMP, NEW YORK STATE LINES; 23" high with immovable handle; 10½" diameter widest base part; burned kerosene. $415.00 up

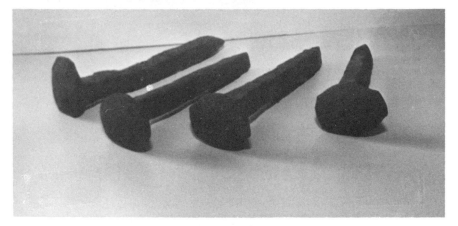

RAILROAD SPIKES
$15.00 each

184

STEAM LOCOMOTIVE BELL, ca. 1890 – 1900. Only the bell is brass; all else including clapper was cast from iron; beautiful tones. Embossed: C.C. 4534 – 12942. $2,200.00 up

BIG BELL from one of the largest steam locomotives once on the Erie Railroad operating all over the system from New York to Chicago; shipping weight 367 lbs.; embossed: MFGd by H.G. HAMMETT, TROY, N.Y., U.S.A. on yoke; since removal from engine, has been painted to protect from damage by exposure. $2,500.00 – $3,000.00 variable

CUSPIDOR (SPITTOON)
Top inside rim granite lined; type seen in railroad station depots and smoking cars as a Victorian effort at public sanitation; 10" high, 9¾" diameter. $45.00

BUGGY STEPS. Buggy – a light 2-wheeled vehicle for one person (two if you didn't mind sitting close) and drawn by one horse. Steps bolted on at a slight angle for rider's balance on getting in as buggy tilted a bit under weight as the foot pressed down, ornamented treads. $45.00 pair

TRADES and COMMERCE

As a good example of one material relying upon another in performance: Razor-sharp CAST IRON BLADE and FITTINGS on an oak frame made this BARREL STAVES CUTTER operable. In a family-trained father to son occupation for several generations on an upstate New York farm. Straight wood staves were cut on this machine and sold to coopers, who in turn heat-bowed and shaped the pieces for making Slack Barrels (to hold apples, onions, potatoes, and the like). Depressing the foot pedal at front raised and lowered the wide cutting knife. (In one of the family's pictures taken of those menfolks stiffly posed in their best "bib and tucker," no hands are visible, each individual having put them into his pockets or behind his back. The reason given was that no one had ten complete fingers; however carefully they fed the wood slantwise into the blade, by the time they got to the short ends of the slabs, finger tips were too often also drawn in.) Today the big tool stands quietly in a corner of the barn active only in gathering cobwebs. $250.00 variable

ANVIL with a heavy "beak," or horn, to balance horseshoes being hammer-shaped to the animal's feet. The farrier was a blacksmith who also shod hooves with iron; this anvil was used bolted into a substantial wood block. Anvils vary considerably. $195.00 – $225.00 and more

This ANVIL whitened from years of accumulated dust in an abandoned farm room. Ca. 1890. Both the army and navy used anvils of this style, theirs weighing up to about 100 lbs., to be carried into the field or for ship-board repairs. Pointed long horn type. $250.00

SALESMAN'S SAMPLE ANVILS
$195.00 – $225.00 each

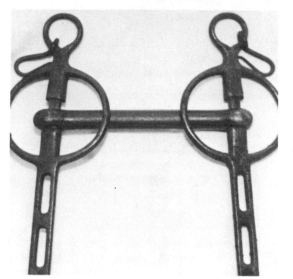

HORSE BRIDLE BIT
Large mouth, both cast and wrought. $75.00 – $95.00

BOTTOM SPREADER or V-FULLER, resembling a cutting hardy; metal can be worked over the edge, spreading rather than cutting it. Maker's touchmark on one end: "A" in a horseshoe. $55.00

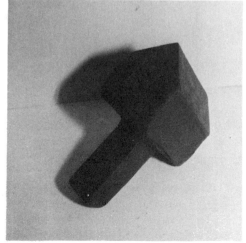

189

BLACKSMITH'S STAND
with cast tools regularly
used: SWAGE BLOCK.
(these weigh 100 to 300
lbs.). FORGE HAMMERS,
SHAPERS, AND CUTTERS.
Tools, $45.00 – $95.00;
Stand, $135.00 +

SLUG CUTTER
Ca. 1895 – 1900; 12½" long; operates by lifting the handle. Maker, H.B.
Rouse & Co., Chicago U.S.A. $75.00 – $95.00

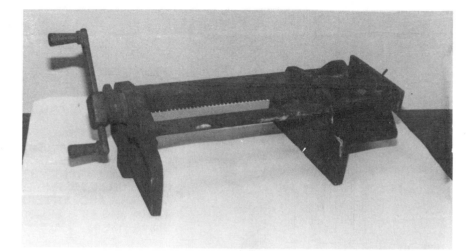

VISE
Embossed: The Columbia Vise & Mfg. Co., Cleveland, O. U.S.A., ca. 1800s.
$125.00

COUNTER SCALE
From an early store at Big Run, Pennsylvania; arm labeled for weighing as: "X dollars for 10 lbs." etc.; embossed: THE COMPUT-ING SCALE CO., DAYTON, OHIO, U.S.A. PATd. 1885; all original. $750.00 variable to area

COFFEE GRINDER
Also from Big Run. Embossed: ENTERPRISE MANUFACTURING CO., PHILADELPHIA, PA.; all original. $695.00 – $775.00 +, more to area

STORE COFFEE GRINDER
Sliding riveted lid; all original; 25½" high x 13" square base, 19½2" diameter each wheel, one with handle; embossed: ENTERPRISE MANUFACTURING CO., PHILADELPHIA, PA., U.S.A. on outer rim of side wheel and at base of grinder; PAT'd May 12, '98 on front of bowl; wood drawer to contain ground coffee. $750.00, more to area

STORE DISPLAY STAND
for CARPET SWEEPERS
Handles kept separately
upright in slots just above
ornately cutout base; front
hooks held hand-pushed
sweepers; still good painted sign BISSELL'S BALL
BEARING; ca. 1926; B.C.
Sweeper Co., Grand
Rapids, Michigan. $195.00
– $225.00

STORE DISPLAY STAND for
CLOTHES WRINGERS
Oak with cast iron fixtures and
base having a gilded horseshoe at
each center with "A W CO." inside
the horseshoes; painted: THE
AMERICAN WRINGER CO.'S
HORSE SHOE BRAND, EVERY
ONE WARRANTED; iron casters.
$195.00 – $225.00

BUGGY WHIP DISPLAY HOLDER: 33¼" wide; 30 separate holding slots; hung high in store to accommodate length of whips. $175.00 – $195.00

Wall DISPLAY RACK embossed: "USE HANDY BOX FRENCH SHOE BLACKING, PATd. September 1, '91; from an old Pennsylvania store; note care given to fanciful design. $195.00 – $225.00

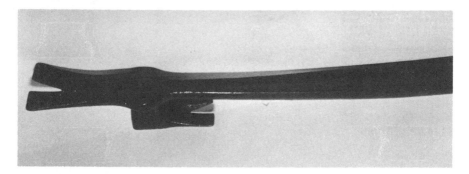

TWO-PURPOSE CRATE OPENER, pry lids and remove fasteners; 13" long; embossed: BUY ONLY ARM & HAMMER SODA. $55.00

BILLING MACHINE
Used paper rolls. $95.00

Embossed: GUMMED PAPER DISPENSER STORE No. 5; small well stores water to moisten paper using roller; Patent dated May 14, 1918. $48.00

PAPER FILE (SPIKE)
7½" high; spike set in raised slot in cutout patterned cast base. $18.00

PAPER SPIKES with embossed designs on bases; spikes added in raised holders; one 6" high; other 7¼" high. $18.00 each
BOTTLE OPENER. $10.00

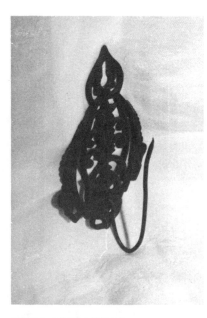

WALL SPIKE (FILE)
Ornate casting with wrought spike. $38.00

CRATE OPENER & HATCHET.
$48.00

COUNTER SCALE
For small purchases; brass arm to 15 lbs.; cast sliding wt.; traces of red and yellow japanned finish. $195.00 – $225.00

BEEHIVE STRINGHOLDER
Fluted edge and grooved "hive"; much copied style; bolted to counter; prices differ a great deal. $95.00

BEEHIVE STRINGHOLDER
Uncommonly handsome design; used bolted to counter; imprinted: PATENTED FEB. 14, 1860. $175.00 – $195.00

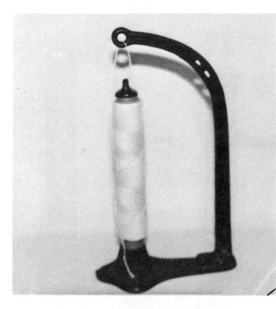

CONE STRINGHOLDER
One of the earlier styles.
$45.00

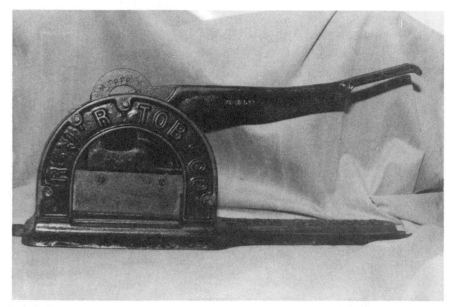

PLUG TOBACCO CUTTER
Bolted to counter; embossed: R. J. REYNOLDS CO., and on arm: BROWN'S MULE. Pulling down the handle lowers sharp blade to cut chaws to order (at first 5 cents ea.); 18½" long x 8" high; original black japanned finish with gold striping; mint condition. $195.00 – $225.00

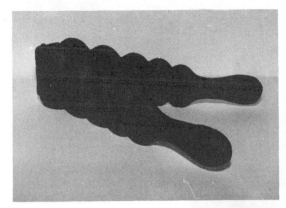

MOLD (opened and closed) for making LEAD SINKER used with fishing lines. $45.00

WINDOW PULLEY embossed: M.W. & CO. NEW HAVEN (Conn.) ca. 1880s. $38.00

TOBACCONIST'S SHOP Rarity: stood on counter, said to hold cigars; embossed: PATd. 1890; Pennsylvania origin; Grecian figure whose raised arms hold turntop plate with "holders." $150.00 – $195.00

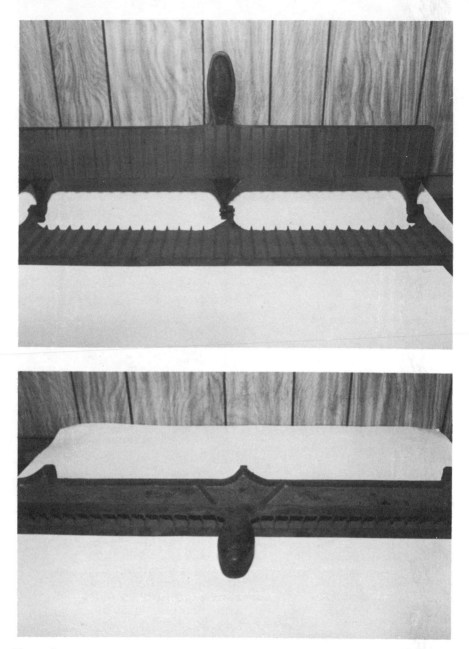

Two views, open and closed, of CANDYMAKER'S CANDY CUTTER; embossed: COLLUM BUTTERCUP CANDY CUTTER for ribbon candy. Dated 1892, 23½" wide. $245.00 – $275.00

CANDY SHOP SCALE
Embossed: ENTERPRISE MANUFACTURING CO., PHILA. PA.; tin
scoop; brass slide. $225.00 – $235.00

**COMMERCIAL BUTTER
ROLLER**
(roller is brass and inside
of handle is wood) ca.:
1850; 7" wide, 10" roller to
tip of handle. $175.00 –
$195.00

COMMERCIAL VEGETABLE SLICER
Ca. 1900 – 1903; Inventor: H. J. Hook, Buffalo, N.Y.; 39" high x 21" overall wide. $195.00

TRADE SIGN or INSUR-ANCE EMBLEM for hanging outside shop; trade sign to advertise, insurance emblem to denote fire protection; Initials L and B in a large B; North Carolina origin; looks like 18th to earliest 19th centuries. $450.00 – $475.00 variable

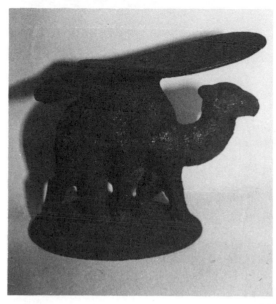

CAMEL DISPLAY STAND
from children's shoe shop.
$85.00

STORE SHOE STRETCHER
Much used in general
stores which had a corner
for shoe sales; primarily
for bunion sufferers;
Embossed 1 side: PATd.
OCT. 12, 1891; Embossed
other side: LIGHT – FUL-
TON, ILL. $45.00

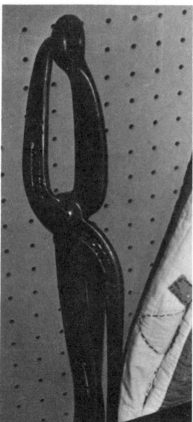

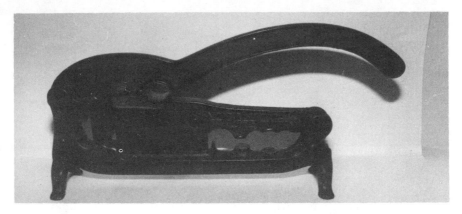

APOTHECARY'S CORKPRESS
Embossed: PAT'd. Jan. 6, 1863, S. LEE, TAUNTON, MASS., ca. 1880. Choosing a cork closest to size needed for medicine container, druggist moistened it, placed it in proper slot and pulled down the handle with considerable pressure. Inserted into the bottle, cork swelled to seal the contents. Tool was used bolted to a counter. $195.00 – $210.00

BARBER'S CHAIR
49" high x 24" wide x 43" deep; porcelain trims with restored leather; from an old Lockport, N.Y. shop; embossed: KOKEN BARBERS SUPPLY CO., ST. LOUIS: operable. $1,500.00 – $1,800.00

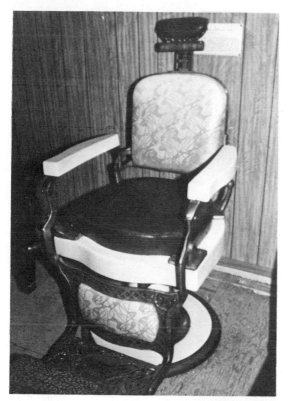

BARBER'S CHAIR
Upholstered sections restored; porcelain trims; embossed: THE E. BERNING-HAUS CO., CINCINNATI, O.; operable. $1,500.00 variable

BARBER'S CHAIR
42" high; seat 18" x 21" deep; Pat. dtd. 1891; maker marked: KOKEN BARBERS SUPPLY CO. ST. LOUIS, U.S.A.; cast iron with oak; restored upholstery; operable. $1,500.00 – $1,800.00 +

BARBER'S CHAIR
Upholstery restored; balance cast iron; embossed ornate Victorian designs; operable; dated 1868; made at Cincinnati, Ohio. $1,800.00 – $2,000.00 variable

MORTARS & PESTLES
Both urn shapes; (inverted bells). Smaller, more difficult to find; 4" high; ca. late 1800s. $125.00 – $145.00. Larger. $125.00 – $145.00 up

MORTARS and PESTLES
From apothecary shops.
Note that one has a masher
at either end of the pestle;
one plain and one grooved
base. $195.00 – $250.00
Lower. $200.00 – $250.00

GROUP of COBBLER'S SHOE LASTS for both men and women; ca. 1850 – 1890. $40.00 each

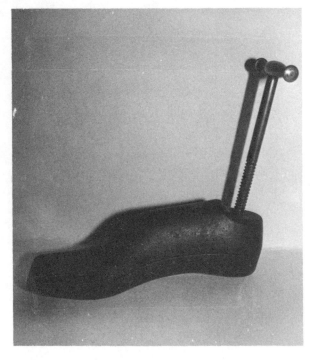

SHOE STRETCHER
Brass handle screwed down to raise the form and give arch relief; ca. 1860. $40.00

COBBLER'S DOUBLE REPAIR FORM
Embossed: IRF & CO., ANNISTON, ALA. $45.00

COBBLER'S EXTRA-HEAVY REPAIR FORM; very old. $60.00

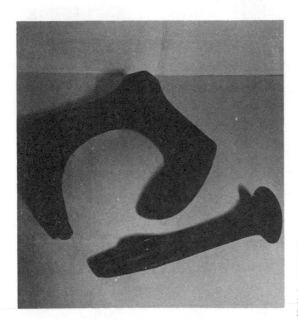

COBBLER'S SHOE REPAIR FORMS (LASTS)
Patents 1884 – 1887 and Applied For: uncommon styles. Pin removal is rare.
$75.00 – $85.00 each

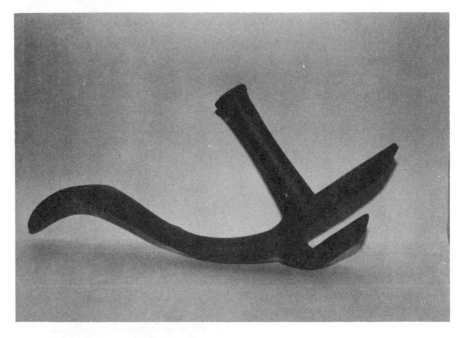

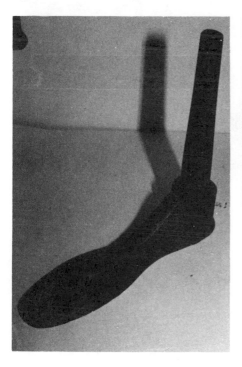

SHOESHINE STAND FOOT REST
4 bolt holes to install on a tall
bench. $42.50

COBBLER'S SHOE LAST
Used with sole of iron foot
up to permit work on soles.
$38.00

LEAD MOLD
Embossed: LYMAN for
maker's identification. Ca.
late 1800s. $55.00 variable

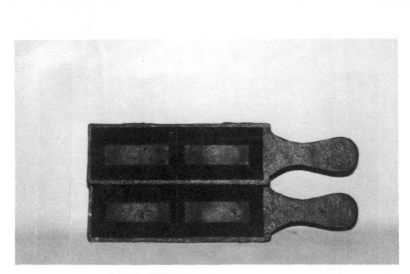

LEAD MOLDS
Unusual with handles; very old. $95.00 pair

LEAD MELTING POT
Heavy wire bail. $45.00

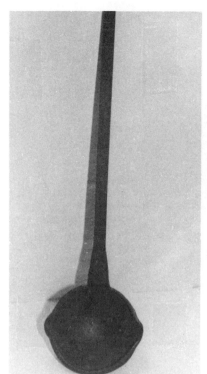

LEAD POURING LADLE
with lips both sides; 11"
long handle; two pcs. cast
and then handle forged
onto bowl casting. $42.50

GLUE MELTING POT
Smaller, holding glue chunks, fits into larger, holding boiling water; heavy
wire bails; imprinted on outside of larger vessel: MARIETTA, PA. Smaller is
white granite lined. $48.00 each

WOOD CLAMPS
Embossed: AUSTIN & EDDY BOSTON PATd. 1886. $75.00 pair

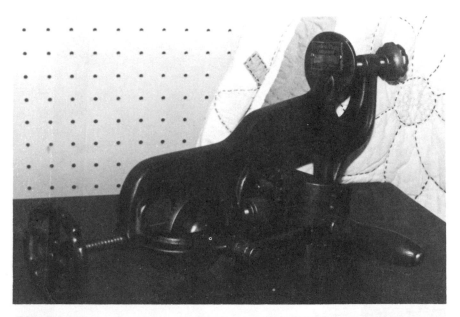

BENCH DRILL. On plate: GOODELL-PRATT COMPANY LOCKSMITHS
GREENFIELD, MASS. U.S.A. PATd. 1895. $125.00 +

PRINTING PRESS, KELSEY & CO., MERIDEN, CONN. U.S.A., 1885; 22" wide, 19" high, 12" deep; used to turn out 5 x 8 calling cards, labels for maple sugar containers, advertisements, and bill headings. $300.00 – $375.00

BOOK BINDER
Panels 20" long, 7" high. $225.00

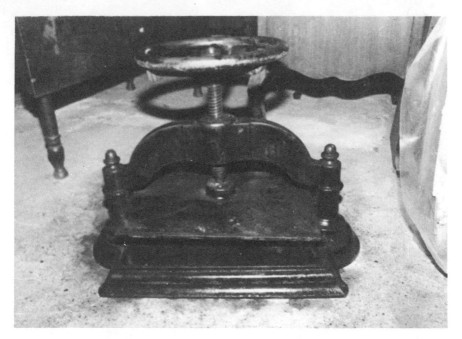

BOOKPRESS, original (worn) japanned black finish with stenciled patterns; operable. $195.00 variable

BOOKPRESS
Polished and finish-treated, operable. $195.00 variable

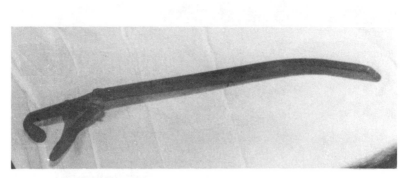

AUTO TIRE CHANGER
Ca. 1920s; took the tire off the rim. $35.00

CAR JACK
Had a handle that fit into square socket. $45.00

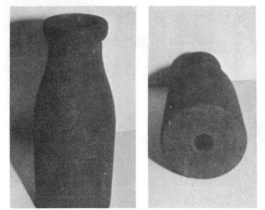

CARNIVAL or COUNTY FAIR TARGET
Set up for "Baseball Throws" as a "Carney Game," when hit with a baseball, the bottle was supposed to fall over, a prize then awarded. Instead, the bottle has a hole in the bottom, and is held with a wooden pin protruding from the game's platform, so it couldn't fall over. $75.00

FAIR AND CARNIVAL SHOOTING GALLERY OR BASEBALL THROW TARGETS (Birds)
Chipped original paint on iron castings; set up in lines in a metal track; when hit, would fall back; prizes for enough hits. $65.00 each

PENNY CIGARETTE MACHINE
10½" high x 9" wide x 8" deep; ca. 1930; Side lever permitted dispensing of Old Gold, Lucky Strike, Wings, Twenty Grand, Kool, Chesterfield, Fatima, Camels, and Helmar. All original and operable. $225.00 +

GUMBALL MACHINE – 1 cent. 15¾" high x 7½" square; complete and original; has key. Embossed: THANK YOU on flap over dispenser slot; maker's STAR and CGI; it works. (These heavily reproduced.) $195.00

GUMBALL MACHINE – 1 cent. Maker marked: Patd. 11-5-1912, 4-24-1923; ADVANCE MACHINE CO., CHICAGO, U.S.A. $195.00 PEANUT DISPENSER – 1 cent. Marked: THE NORTHWESTERN CORP., MORRIS. Both operable. $195.00

WEAPONS AND RELATED ITEMS

CONFEDERACY ARTILLERY GRAPE SHOT STAND (Civil War – 1861 – 1865) Excavated at Blakely Battlefield, Alabama (across the river from Mobile), a RARITY. 9 small cannonballs held together in one loose unit by a shaft with iron plates top and bottom. When a cannon was fired, the shaft broke, releasing the entire unit, as seen here, from the cannon's muzzle, much like a shotgun blast. $950.00 – $1,000.00

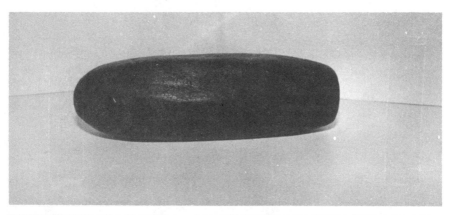

"WHITWORTH" PROJECTILE used by CONFEDERATE ARTILLERY, A RARITY. Whitworth Armament Co., Birmingham, England, sold our Confederacy one of the few breechloading cannon types used during the Civil War, unusual in their day with a "rifled" bore, the projectiles rifled to match the bore. $400.00+

PAIR of CONFEDERATE HAND GRENADES (RARITIES)
Found at the location of the Southern Forces foundry at Selma, Alabama, where they were manufactured during the Civil War. Holes for insertion of fuses. (Hand grenades were heavily used for siege operations.) $425.00 up pair

SHELL LOADER
2 pcs. joined with pin; handles' undersides hollow. $55.00

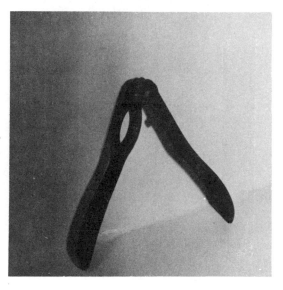

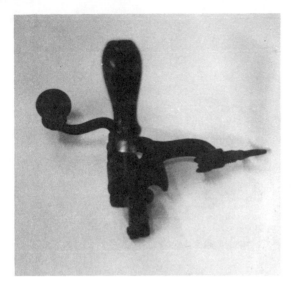

SHELL LOADER
Clamps on a board; brass
ferrule; wood handlegrips.
$55.00 +

SHELL LOADER
Table clamp; wood handlegrips. $55.00 +

MOLD
For 2 separate shot sizes
and shapes; heavy. $58.00 +

BRANDING IRON
Cast and forged; Horse
Cavalry, U.S. $250.00 up

Schroeder's
ANTIQUES
Price Guide . . . is the #1 bestselling
antiques & collectibles value guide on the market today,
and here's why . . .

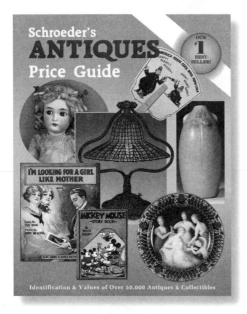

8½ x 11 • 608 Pgs. • PB • $14.95